I Ran to Alva

I Ran to Alva

By

Jack Randy Martin

I Ran to Alva, Edition II

ISBN-13: 978-1490420523

ISBN-10: 1490420525

Contents

I Ran to Alva

A Journey's Harbinger

The rising sun was a welcome sight to Mel as he looked across the jagged peaks to the east. He thought he'd have better luck staying awake with some scenery to look at instead of darkness, and Wyoming had more than its share of the former. This particular highway tended generally east and west, but it sure had a habit of wandering every direction on the compass. On one of the few straight sections of road, he took a second to look at the GPS and determine how far he still had to go. Hmmmm…an hour or so. He reasoned that it was unlikely they'd already be awake so early on a Saturday morning, so it made little sense for him to push through. He was getting dangerously drowsy and if he showed up in a sleep deprived stupor, he might seem a bit strange to his new employer.

It took ten more minutes to find a place along the road that was flat and wide enough to accommodate his crew cab pickup and massive 5th wheel trailer. He pulled over cautiously and brought the rig to a stop. The diesel engine shut down with a shudder, as though relieved to be done with its work. He set the parking brake, crawled over the front seat to the back, then zipped the sleeping bag wide open and laid it over him as he reclined. It was obvious that a pillow would be nice, so he balled up a sweatshirt and tucked it under his head. Sleep came quickly……..

For an hour.

He was startled awake by the sharp sound of metal rapping against the window above his head. He lurched to a sitting position, bewildered and irritated at the man standing outside the truck tapping the Maglite against the glass.

"Knock it off! You're gonna break the damn window!" he shouted to the man. At that, his blurry eyes finally got a good look at the uniformed officer. He was at least 6'3", broad shouldered, barrel chested and probably 60 years old. "Ohhh, oh I am sorry......." He spoke loud enough to be heard through the glass.

"Roll down the window please," the officer commanded.

He complied and greeted him awkwardly, "Good morning officer, I was..."

"License and registration please, sir," the officer commanded.

Flustered, he clumsily retrieved his wallet, extracted the license, and handed it to the officer. "I have to get into my glove box for the registration," he said, nodding toward the front of the cab.

"Certainly," the stoic officer replied.

He climbed over the seat to the front and, after much shuffling of papers, was able to find the truck and trailer registrations. He handed them over uneasily as well and then waited for the officer to tell him the nature of his visit.

"Dominic Melvin Hatcher of Los Angeles, Cal-i-fornnnnnyaaaaaaa" the officer said, dragging it out as if it was some contemptible name he didn't want to speak.

"Yes sir...".

"Mr. Hatcher," the officer paused deliberately, "I stopped to check on you because the tire on your trailer's left rear axle is absolutely shredded."

"Huh? I mean, it is?"

"Yes sir. There's hardly any rubber left on the rim at all. You didn't hear it blow or feel the trailer towing in any peculiar manner?"

"No sir, I didn't notice a thing."

"Have you had anything to drink in the last several hours, Mr. Hatcher? Alcoholic beverages, I mean".

"No sir. Actually, I seldom drink."

"Let me smell your breath." The officer leaned in toward him and Mel exhaled directly into his face. "Hmm, well I don't detect any controlled substances in your breath, Mr Hatcher, but I must say I am a bit surprised you didn't hear that tire blow or notice the trailer towing funny."

"I'm just really tired, sir."

"Then you should have pulled over sooner, Mr. Hatcher. You might have killed someone with this rig of yours if you fell asleep at the wheel."

"Yes sir."

"Do you have a spare for that trailer and do you know how to change it?"

"Yes on both counts."

"Uh-huh. Well, where are you goin'?"

"Alva."

"Alva?" the officer seemed surprised. "How does someone from Los Angeles know anyone in Alva?"

"I'm going there for a job on a ranch. I found them on the internet while I was doing a job search. I haven't met them yet. It's my first time up here."

"Well you get yourself some more sleep and then you fix that tire. You don't look too alert to me."

"Yes sir."

The officer's posture relaxed just a tad as he handed the papers back to Mel. "Go in to Ruby's Diner in Hulett for some breakfast. Tell Ruby that Dean said hello."

"Oh, oh, yeah, yes, I sure will. Dean?"

"*She* calls me Dean."

"Ahh, yes sir, Officer…." He hesitated and looked at the officer's name tag and examined his uniform a little more closely, "…oh, I mean Deputy Peterson. I will be sure to speak to Ruby."

"*Sheriff* Peterson. Very well." He walked to his patrol car and drove hastily away.

Mel laid down to resume his sleep. It took a few minutes, but he managed to doze off and slept comfortably for a couple more hours. Eventually he was awakened by……What the hell was that noise? It was like someone blowing through a kid's toy horn.

He sat up and peered out all the windows. There, about 100 feet from the passenger side of the truck, a Bull Elk stood with his head in the air, "bugling" as they call it, in his call for a mate. "Awesome," Mel said aloud as a smile crossed his face. It felt like a good sign, like a harbinger, a welcome call. "Maybe this wasn't such a crazy decision after all," he muttered to himself.

He was rested enough to get moving again, so he put on a warm sweatshirt and went back to assess the blown trailer tire. He had the spare on in a few minutes, but was wondering if there were any tire shops in Hulett or Alva to buy a replacement. He cleaned his hands with the container of Baby Wipes he always kept in the tool box and got back in the truck. The big diesel rumbled to life and Mel eased the whole rig out onto the road. The digital dash clock said 9:30am and his stomach was grumbling loudly. He hoped Hulett wasn't too far down the road, as the GPS was having trouble acquiring a signal.

He soon passed the Welcome to Hulett sign and began looking for Ruby's. The bridge crossing the Belle Fourche River was kinda neat and the town was built for real on the other side. Charming town, he thought, definitely a bit sleepier than LA and that would be a welcome change. He wondered about the kids who grew up here, probably complained constantly that there was "nothing to do" and they'd leave as soon as they could. He knew that story, and right now he would run straight back to Oklahoma if things were different. Hometowns like Hulett, thought Mel, became a part of someone that they didn't know was there until they left it for a while. Then that town they spent their whole life escaping became the one place on earth they really wanted to be. A lucky few sometimes made it back on their own terms. For those who didn't, the little home town became their favorite vacation destination and the core of their fondest memories. Mel didn't know if this place would be what he needed, but he figured it was a damn sight better than what he'd left. And for now, that was all he needed to know.

I Ran to Alva

Ruby's

Mel spotted Ruby's Diner on the opposite side of the road and decided to park somewhere on this side and then walk across. One clear drawback to his truck and trailer was the room needed to park or turn around, so he'd learned to pick his spots carefully. The locals sitting near the diner's windows didn't pay too much attention, as rigs like his were commonplace in town, owing to the close proximity of the Devil's Tower. The popular tourist attraction was visited by multitudes of RV'ers and many of them came through Hulett.

Ruby's was everything Mel expected a small town diner to be; casual, rural, and lots of historical nick-nacks and photos. It also smelled wonderfully and was clean as a whistle. Predictably, it was filled with the din of conversation, clinking dishes and cups and ventilation motors humming above the grills.

"Come on down here honey," a sixty-something woman called to him. She was waving and flashing a big smile. He walked past the end of the counter and took his place at the only remaining table. He noticed "Ruby" on her polished gold name tag and returned her friendly greeting.

"Busy place," he observed in an affirming tone.

"Busiest time of day, honey. You're lucky to have a seat this time on a Saturday."

"Well, that's great 'cuz I'm starving."

"We can sure fix that problem for you, but you'll have to solve the rest of 'em on your own," she said with a wink.

Mel liked her immediately. There was something absolutely genuine about her. He figured she'd grown up in this town and knew every local who had ever lived within a 50 mile radius. She could probably tell a 5-minute story about every photograph on the wall and every person occupying a seat. - except for out of towners of course. And even though he was one, she didn't make him feel that way. "Oh, Dean says hello."

"Ahh,"she smiled,"he did, did he? Did you meet him in an official capacity?"

"Yes, but he was just checking on me. I pulled over to get some sleep and as he patrolled past, he noticed one of the tires on my trailer had blown apart, so he stopped to advise me on it. He was cool. Told me to get some more sleep and then fix the tire before moving on. That's when he told me about your place."

"He was cool?" she seemed surprised.

"Yep. Very official and all, but pretty cool."

"Hmm, you must have caught him in a good mood."

"Oh?"

"This is friendly country, but Dean – Sheriff Peterson – ain't exactly Andy Griffith."

"Yeah I sorta got that."

"So what are you doin' around here, honey, just passin' through?

"Actually, no. I am starting work Monday on a ranch over in Alva."

"Really? Whose?"

"Terri Green's"

"Hmmmmm, not sure I know that name. Hey Sam?" she called to the nearest cook. "Do you know a ranch over in Alva owned by a Terri Green?"

The elderly cook thought a moment. "Weaverly's old place." He answered without even looking back.

"Ohhhhhh, sure, nice place. I've yet to meet her but have heard talk. Small towns, you know? Kind of a serious young woman, not a lot of time for chit chats. And speaking of... I should probably be getting your order. D'ya know what you want?"

"Oh, just a couple eggs and a stack of pancakes, and start me off with some coffee."

"Sure honey, comin' right up." She said cheerfully and hustled off to do a thousand other tasks.

Mel sat quietly at the little dinette and stared at the pics adorning the wall. Many were black and white, some had dates and places written on them, most signed to Ruby with a brief note of thanks. He even spotted one with a much-younger Ruby riding a tall Appaloosa through a stream. This wall is probably her photo album, he thought. All her friends, family, history right out here for all to enjoy and be a part of, not tucked away in a book inside a coffee table. He thought that was kinda cool.

Just then he heard the little door-mounted brass bell call out brightly as it had done when he walked into the place. Immediately after, there was a notable reduction in noise and conversation in the diner. The change caught Mel's attention and he looked toward the door to see what or who had muffled the crowd. Three men about Mel's age had walked in; the largest of the three was in front and clearly was the focus of most peoples' attention. Mel watched as the large man bent over and engaged a seated patron in what appeared to be a rather tense conversation. After a few seconds, the large man stood up and began scanning the diner as though he was looking for someone in particular. Apparently, he was looking for Mel…

As soon as Mel and the other man made eye contact, he began walking in Mel's direction. His face looked purposeful, not friendly, and Mel knew that a confrontation of unknown origin was about to take place.

"You there," the man said when he got near," you driving that Ford with the trailer?"

"Yes. Is there a problem?" Mel answered as evenly and smoothly as he could.

"Sure is, Mr California," he said in obvious reference to the license plates, "that overgrown tourist wagon is taking up about three parking spaces. Me and my buddies had to park around the corner."

"Yeah, well when I parked there it was wide open, there was no one around. It looked like a good spot."

"It is a good spot, Hollywood, and that's why I usually park there. Only I couldn't this particular morning because your piece of shit is taking up all the real estate."

Mel noted that the man had begun to raise his voice and his posture reflected a rising aggression. This was likely to get ugly, but Mel really wasn't afraid of the slightly larger man. He was no stranger to rough and tumble situations himself. He became aware of the diner patrons' focus and the steadily diminishing noise level.

"Well, I'll be out of here as soon as I eat and…" Mel's snarky side rose up…"peace and harmony will be restored to your universe."

"You some kind of smartass?" the man replied, practically spitting the words, as he stepped to within arm's reach of Mel.

"Yeah, sometimes."

"I have a way of dealing with smartasses, mister and you're about to find out."

"DYLAN TURNER!!!!" Ruby screamed through the diner. "You will behave yourself in my place! Do you understand?!?!"

"I understand I'm about to wipe your floor with this guy's ass, Ruby. Hey, you know what?" he turned his attention back to Mel, "I think Ruby here likes you. Weird, but I think she does. So I'm gonna make you a deal."

"What's that, big guy?" replied Mel, deliberately sounding bored.

"You go out and move your rig right now and I won't trash her diner while I put a beatdown on you."

"Gee, what a tempting offer, " Mel replied flatly as he had already measured the distance of the big man's groin to be well within striking range. At that moment, he caught a look at Ruby and saw the stress on her face. She had certainly slowed the man down, but was not going to be able to stop him. Mel wondered about her place getting trashed and wondered how many of the patrons in here he was going to see again, and have to get along with. He was aware of the big man's two buddies still standing near the door. Mel was certain he could handle...Dylan....but at what price to the diner? And could he handle three men? Probably not. "Allright....because Ruby is so nice to me, and because you present such a compelling case with your backup squad over there, I'll go move the rig."

"I don't need no backup squad, Hollywood."

"OK, fine." Mel gestured to Dylan, indicating that he was going to stand up, but could not do so with him standing so close. "Do you want me to move the rig or not?"

Dylan backed up enough to give him room to stand and took stock of him for the brief moment they stood shoulder to shoulder. The tourist was only an inch or two shorter and while he looked maybe 30 pounds lighter, he was also in excellent physical condition. He could probably put up a good fight, Dylan thought, if he only had the heart. "Anywhere is fine!" he taunted Mel "Just not where it is," he finished with a laugh.

Mel stared straight at the door as he walked through the diner, aware of the eyes upon him. No doubt those eyes were full of pity, for this certainly could not have been the first time they'd seen the bully in action. The two bookends, as Mel thought of them, stood near the door and smirked as he walked past. Now these guys, Mel thought, haven't an ounce of fight in them. They are Dylan's lackies, his coattail riders, hanging just close enough to the boss to hopefully look cool. Mel winked and smiled at one of them as he passed, setting the hook for a future engagement he figured would come. He walked across the street, climbed into the truck and dutifully moved it around the corner and to a vacant lot that used to be home to a gas station.

The short walk back to the diner probably wouldn't be a waste, he thought, as it would have taken time to cook his breakfast anyway. It occurred to him that Dylan and the bookends would probably be occupying his table when he returned, so he needed to mentally plan for that. No biggie, he thought, just don't give them the satisfaction of seeing the look of surprise on his face. True to form, when Mel walked back into Ruby's, he looked across the diner and there they were, the three of them, yucking it up at his table. An elderly couple sitting at a 4-seat booth offered him a place to sit with them and he graciously accepted. They reminded him just a little of his deceased grandparents and he knew he would feel comfortable in their presence while making idle conversation about the weather and what not.

Ruby caught his eye, nodded, and brought his breakfast in just another minute. "I'm sorry, honey, but thank you for handling that the way you did. That man has been trouble for years."

"Not at all, Ruby. I've met his type before. He actually likes intimidating people more than physically beating them. I just gave him what he wanted."

Ruby was struck by the easy confidence with which Mel expressed himself and she realized he spoke the truth. He was not at all afraid of Dylan Turner. And looking at him, the boy was stout. It occurred to her that he had indeed done her a favor. He backed down not to save his own skin, but to spare her the trauma of a brawl inside her place. What a sweet boy, she thought.

Mel enjoyed his breakfast in the company of the elderly couple who regaled him with tales of Hulett and Alva back in the old days. They talked about the cattle drives in which the herds were driven right through town to the railroad stockyard. It all sounded like stories from the Wild Wild West, but it was just before WWII, a time most people really consider "modern." But as they told him, fewer than 20 people in town had telephone service at that time and less than half had electricity. They seemed interested in his picking up and moving from LA to come work on a ranch, but cautioned him that winters up here were sure to be rougher than what he'd experienced in California.

After about a half hour, Dylan and the bookends walked past on their way out.

"Enjoy your drive back to "Cali"…dude," Dylan said, "and tell Angelina I said hey."

"I won't be going back to Cali…..I'm moving here." Mel replied flatly.

"Oh? Well, whaddaya know? Didja come up here to make movies?" Dylan joked, slapping one of the bookends on the shoulder to elicit an obligatory laugh.

"Nothing that fancy. Just taking a job on a ranch."

"You don't say? Well, don't hurt yourself doing real work. I'll be seein ya around, Hollywood. Be careful where you park." With that, he and the bookends exited the diner.

"I knew that boy's granddad and his father," the old man said to Mel. "Grandad was a good man, but his father…he was a wild one. Spent some time in Rawlins, he did."

"Rawlins?"

"State Penitentiary. I think he robbed a bank and pistol whipped a security guard. Yeah, I believe that's right," as his wife nodded affirmation. "Dylan was a big shot football hero around here, got himself a scholarship to…..Montana State, I think it was."

"What happened with that?"

"As I heard it, he just pissed it all away with partying and panty-chasing. Didn't study, flunked out. No other school would touch him. So he comes back home and works at his uncle's lumber mill these last 8 – 10 years, whatever it's been. And he just turned into the nastiest bully. A bitter young man, takes his troubles out on everyone else."

Mel listened intently to the background info, certain that at some point it might become useful if he stayed around here long enough. Finally, he took note of the clock on the wall and figured 11:00 was plenty late enough to go meet his new employer.

I Ran to Alva

The Grizzled Veteran Rancher

Traffic was surprisingly brisk for such a rural area and Mel had to pick just the right moment to pull the big truck and trailer into the flow on Highway 24 toward Alva. Once rolling, he was able to enjoy the countryside, rejuvenated as he was by the scrumptious breakfast and coffee. The road followed the general path of a creek in the lowest part of the valley for about a dozen miles until he reached the county road turn. Along the way, bucolic farms and ranches were situated at the bases of the hills and cliffs in a way that would do a Thomas Kincade painting proud. He drove along at faster pace than he wanted to keep from holding everyone up on the two lane road where passing spots were few.

The turn onto County Road 54 revealed it to be a typical rural farm road. - rolling, bumpy with turns that suddenly got sharper, and with no posted speed limits. His 5th wheel could easily get him in trouble on this asphalt ribbon, so he took it real easy. The GPS's feminine British voice spoke out the declining mileage numbers to his destination as his anticipation began to build. "You have reached your destination" she informed him as he passed a rather prominent fence and creek crossing, but there was no driveway to be seen. He figured he must have reached the property line recognized by the GPS software, so he kept a sharp eye along the right side of the road for any evidence of a driveway or dwelling. After at least another half mile, he spotted a collection of buildings up ahead and began to slow down. Sure enough, the large, post-mounted mail box had the correct address numbers, so he pulled the rig in and looked for a good place to park. He stopped just shy of the barn and let the diesel go to rest. Once it was quiet, he noticed there were no dogs barking and circling the truck. He thought that was rather peculiar. Every farm or ranch he'd ever set foot on had dogs. How did you run one without them? Hmmmm.

He stepped out of the truck, looked around for a few seconds, straightened his shirt and started to walk toward the house.

"We're in here." A female voice called out from inside the barn.

"OK" Mel replied and walked to the open double door entry. The woman who called to him was about his age but the man at her side was much older than he had anticipated. They were kneeling next to a Palomino mare lying on her side and in obvious distress.

"She was due two days ago," the older man stated without even looking at Mel, "but she can't push. That foal is stuck up in there real good like. This is bad."

"The vet in Hulett says he thinks the foal is breech, but the vet broke his leg last week and can't come out." The woman added.

"Breech, huh?" Mel asked.

"Yeah, that means…" the older man began

"That its butt is facing out…yes, I know." Mel affirmed. "Saw this a time or two on my Grampa's place. He even showed me how to help the mare, but it was a few years ago."

"Well, it sounds like you are the only one here with any experience at all," she continued tersely. "Whatever you know, could you try it now? If we can't help her, we'll lose them both."

Mel removed his outer shirt and then also pulled the sleeve up a bit on the left arm of his t-shirt. "Get her attention with some treats or water or something and hold her down. She ain't gonna like this." He walked over to a water outlet and rinsed off his exposed left arm.

The woman moved to a position directly in front of the mare's face and began talking to her in smooth, hushed tones. The older man gingerly grabbed a handful of the halter on the backside of her head and prepared his grip while positioning himself to throw his weight on the mare should she try to rise. He knew what the younger man was about to do.

Mel knelt down behind the mare and slowly inserted his hand into her birth canal and moved gently further up to the foal. The mare indeed protested and twice tried to rise, but the man and woman did their job well and managed to restrain her movements. Mel was finally able to feel the butt of the foal and could tell that its rear legs had folded forward, creating an ever-widening wedge of a body trying to push its way out – and that was never going to work. It would die in there and kill the mare through sepsis. Recalling his grampa's coaching, he reached further up and found the foal's rear hooves. He bent them at the ankles toward the rear, and then pushed up to force the knees to bend as far as possible. Now for the tricky part.

Keeping constant pressure on the foal's lower legs, he began pulling the hooves toward him and the birth canal. The foal panicked at the contact and began thrashing which caused the mare to jolt in turn. "Lay on her!" Mel called to the elderly man.

"I's tryin' dammit!"

They were just able to subdue the mare and keep her down, so Mel was able to resume. He had not released his grip on the foal's hooves and so he began pulling on them again. This time the foal resisted only a little and Mel was able to slowly extend its legs straight out, much to the discomfort of the grunting, wide-eyed mare. At last the rear hooves were visible and in another few seconds the mare had a heavy contraction, exposing the remainder of the legs. Soon she experienced another one and Mel was able to assist the little colt into the world to see his mama for the first time. It had been more than a decade since he'd last done that, but evidently the lesson had stuck, as most lessons did with him. The three stood back from the mare and her newborn colt to let them get acquainted.

"You....must be Melvin," the woman said, extending her hand and smiling just a little. "I'm Terri. I know I kinda already gave you the job, but.... I certainly won't be changing my mind. "Lester..." She continued, looking at the other man.

"Oh! I'm Lester! I didn't mean to yell at ya there son, I's just a little skeered is all," he said, extending his hand and showing a big, gap toothed smile. Lester appeared to be one of those stereotypical, life long ranch hands. He was probably 65, lean and sinewy with hands like leather and an easy going demeanor. He reminded Mel of several men that had worked on his Grampa's huge ranch where he had grown up in Oklahoma, and Mel had liked them all. There was nothing complicated or haughty about them. They worked hard, had simple tastes in life, were mostly honest and didn't give a rat's ass what other people thought of them.

"No problem, it was kinda tense. Pretty cool, though, huh? I was only out of my truck 2 minutes and walked into this….You guys have this much action going on all the time? I might have to ask for more money." He smiled.

Lester chuckled. "Good luck with that one, son."

Terri instructed Lester to keep an eye on the mare and the new colt while she and Mel discussed the basics of everything. They walked out of the barn together. She was not very much like Mel imagined her to be through her emails. She was perhaps a little taller than average, appeared to be full figured, though it was hard to tell with her loose fitting jeans and flannel shirt. Her manner of communication had suggested she was a straight-to-the-point type, and his original perception was that she was sort of an "office manager' kind of rancher/farmer who ran things via computer and merely barked instructions at the hired hands all day. Time would reveal if that impression was accurate or not. Between her floppy hat and the hair dangling around her face, it was difficult to tell what her eyes looked like because she seldom held still for very long.

"I'd like you to park your rig…..wow….that is some trailer….anyway, park it over there on the other side of that large shed. The shed has an electrical outlet and water supply you can plug into and also has a cleanout access for the septic tank where you can attach to the lines."

"Sure, no problem."

"I want you to review the things I said in my emails about living out here, allright? The stuff I said about drugs, drinking, all that. You have a computer, yes?"

"Yes, a laptop."

"Fine. Well, I have wireless internet that you are welcome to use, but if you go bogging me down with movie downloads and such, I will cut you off."

"Got it." He was a little taken aback at her direct and almost indifferent approach to him, given what he had just done in his first 30 minutes. He wasn't the type to expect a ticker-tape parade, but it was almost like the breech birth thing had never happened.

"If you have a printer, I'd like you to print out that one email I sent where I laid out the rules of behavior and then sign it somewhere and give it to me."

"Yes, I have a…"

"Good," she interrupted. "Now I won't expect you to help around here today, given that it's already half gone….and…." she almost grudgingly acknowledged, "what you've already done. So, spend today and tomorrow getting yourself situated and we'll start in for real on Monday."

"Fair enough," Mel replied. He was a bit disappointed in Terri, on a personal level. Sure, her emails had been pretty much to the point, but they did not reveal the terse woman before him. He had grown to know country people, women in particular, as hard working and sober, but also somewhat light hearted and engaging. Terri was…jaded. Like women he'd known in LA. How weird, he thought, but yes, she was like them. She kept herself at least two arms' length distance as they walked, spoke in deliberate tones and never made eye contact. With her floppy hat pulled way down on her forehead, it was hard to tell if she was pretty or not. It shouldn't matter, Mel thought, since she was his employer. He was, after all, a young man and he had gleaned from their online communications that she was somewhere around his age. It was only natural that he'd be curious about her appearance. So her terse disposition and complete lack of interest in displaying any feminine qualities made it comically clear to Mel that he wouldn't be sleeping with the boss to advance his "career."

So the new boss was somewhat of a dichotomy. Jaded like a city girl, uncomplicated like a country girl. In her emails, she had revealed that she'd been on this place less than two years and needed experienced people who wouldn't require much guidance or instruction to get things done. There had to be a story there, but given the indifferent demeanor she had thus far exhibited, Mel wasn't particularly interested in digging into it.

He walked the site where Terri told him to park, then fired up the truck and maneuvered the rig into place with guidance from Lester. After a couple small adjustments, he was happy with its placement, so he disconnected them and then parked the truck behind the trailer, more or less out of sight of the driveway. It took him only another half hour to level it, hook up the water, sewer and electricity. Lester watched with amusement at the speed with which Mel performed the tasks. Clearly, he'd done it many times. Then Lester saw something he hadn't seen before.

Mel walked to the rear of the trailer, turned a couple of fixtures with a key and then pressed a button. An electric motor began whirring and the entire rear panel of the trailer folded down like a huge ramp. Lester was flabbergasted. When the ramp got low enough, he could see there was a room separated from the rest of the trailer. And inside....what the hell? An ATV and a motorcycle! Lester didn't personally know anyone who had so many toys as this young ranch hand Terri hired from California. He was beginning to have his doubts if the young man would work out. Must have got money from his daddy, no doubt. Sure, he handled that breech foal just fine, but that wasn't necessarily hard work, just smart work. He was wondering how Mel would handle hard work.

When the ramp was all the way down, Mel walked up into the open space, unhooked the large side-by-side ATV from the ratcheting tie-downs, released the parking brake, rolled it down the ramp and parked it next to the trailer. He then turned his attention to the motorcycle inside. He similarly released it from the tie-downs and carefully rolled it backwards down the ramp. He parked it next to the ATV and then blanketed it with a special cover he retrieved from a storage compartment. A rather flashy looking bicycle and some exercise equipment were also in the room, but Mel left them there. Then he pressed the same button on the side of the trailer and Lester grinned as he watched the motorized ramp raise itself back into position.

"You got you some toys there, son." He commented.

"Oh I suppose, but this is all I have. I sold everything else when I decided to move. Not a ton of cash in reserves, either," answering the question he knew the elder man wanted to ask.

"Oh, hey 'taint none of my business, no sir…"

"That's allright. I know how it must look. I guy like me showing up for a ten dollar an hour job in a rig like this. It looks odd."

Lester just shrugged.

"I'm gonna spend the rest of the day getting everything set up, but I might want to take the motorcycle out for a little sight seeing tomorrow. Any suggestions?

Lester thought a moment, "How many hours you wanna ride?"

"Most of the day I guess, figure maybe 6 or 8 hours of actual ride time."

"Oh," Lester seemed surprised. So the two men spent the next 10 minutes discussing highways, byways and landmarks to see.

Mel got excited just thinking about it. New roads, new scenery, a new beginning. Then he got an idea. "Hey Lester, how 'bout we get in the ATV and you give me a tour of the ranch?"

"Ahh, well why not? Sure, there's some places and things around here that you oughta know about. Let's go." Lester was a bit giddy as they climbed in the big ATV and started out. It took almost two hours to tour the 3000 acre spread, with Lester giving a narrative as they rolled. Terri was standing near Mel's trailer when they rolled up.

Mel had barely shut the engine down when Terri asked, "You didn't startle the cattle with that thing, did you?"

"No Terri. I drove slowly and quietly. I realize cattle can be skittish, I grew up around them." He wondered how it was possible that this seemingly intelligent woman watched him turn a breeched foal just a few hours ago and was now admonishing him like an ignorant 12 year old. Sure hope this gets better, he thought.

I Ran to Alva

The Team

As May turned to June, the cool mornings and warm afternoons gave way to warm mornings and afternoons that made people wish they'd already done their outdoor work. Mel and Lester needed only a couple weeks to settle into a work routine where each was glad to have the other. Mel appreciated Lester's experience, his easygoing demeanor and most of all, his ability to talk to the mercurial "Miss Terri" without getting ruffled. Lester was glad to have Mel's youth and strength around for the "big stuff", but more importantly his willingness to learn and to work hard without any attitude. Slowly, Lester was able to teach Mel the things that would need attention hourly, daily or weekly. They worked out a pattern by which each man developed preferences for this task or that and within a few weeks the two men ran the ranch like a well-oiled machine.

Lester soon acquired a new favorite part to his day; taking the hay out to the cattle in the far pasture. The herd was only about 350 head, small by ranching standards, and could have subsisted just fine on the grasses during the summer months. It was upon Lester's advice that Terri consented to feed them a small amount of hay to boost their immune and digestive systems. So each day, they scattered a few bales for the bovines. Lester and Mel would throw the hay into the low flatbed trailer and use Mel's big ATV to drag it out for the feeding. Previously, Lester had to hoist the hay up into his old Dodge truck and then endure the non-stop bumping and bouncing for the quarter-mile ride. The ride back was even worse once the truck was empty, but Mel's ATV just floated over the ground like a magic carpet and it pulled that trailer like nothing. Riding across the open land was a joy in this machine. And sometimes when Terri wasn't around, he and Mel would unhitch the trailer and slip over to the far corner of the ranch where the creek ran through. There were multiple places shallow enough to run through the creek, usually at a brisk pace. Lester felt like a kid when the water just splashed up all around, often coming down on them as the vehicle was going fast enough to catch up to its own airborne wake. Who needed amusement park rides?

Their ability to gel as a team had another benefit. It freed Terri to perform the necessities to secure steady customers. Mel and Lester working well together was fine, but without customers to buy the eggs, the produce and the livestock, it was all for naught. She was able to do most of her negotiations and contracts via computer in the small office located at the house's front corner. She had deliberately chosen that room for the office because it had a nearly unrestricted view of the ranch operations thanks to windows on two walls. She had put nearly all her eggs in this particular basket, as it were, and was not about to leave anything to chance. Anyone who worked for her was going to know that she could peer out the window at any moment to monitor what was being done or, just as importantly, not being done. Mel and Lester's work ethic made it possible for Terri to merely compose a list of tasks, (separated into three columns; today, tomorrow, this week), set it on the front porch post under a decorative tiny brass anvil and let the two men handle it each day.

The routine was predictable and steady. Lester always showed up at the crack of dawn, his old Dodge truck rumbling and creaking up the long driveway. He'd stop at the front porch, retrieve the list and then park next to Mel's trailer. Mel always stepped out the moment he heard the truck, two coffees in hand. The two men would sit at the little table under the awning, sip the coffee, review the list and decide how to attack it. The few times Terri watched them from inside the house, she could tell they got along really well, and it seemed Lester enjoyed saying things that made Mel roll his eyes or throw his arms out in mock protest. Then whoever was holding the list would playfully throw it at the other. She knew Lester had never had a son and wondered if maybe that was why he took to Mel so fast. Clearly Lester saw something in him that made it easy to form a friendship. And Mel was easygoing wasn't he? Lester had nothing but praise for his work, unlike the two previous hands who had lasted only about three months each. He never had a cross word, never protested to Terri about anything, he wasn't loud or rude or unkempt. In fact, it occurred to her that he didn't really talk to her that much. Now that was a thought. He was so easygoing and jovial around Lester, but so….businesslike and formal when talking to her. Why was that, she wondered? He hardly seemed like the type to be intimidated by anyone, not even someone who was his employer. Maybe he was just shy around women, she thought. Probably so, but she wondered if maybe she should make some sort of gesture to let him know he was welcome here. Nothing too big, just an informal ice breaking sort of thing. She'd have to consider that.

The corner office room had another effect. The two men were well aware that she might look out at them anytime. Occasionally, they'd see her standing in the window but they never looked directly at her. They just kept working, each joking to the other that the warden was watching. Lester didn't mind really, he understood that she was still pretty new at all this and was determined to make a go of it. Yeah, she was kind of tightly wrapped about how things went on around here, but that was just part of the deal. If you accept her pay, you accept her conditions. When the day comes you no longer can, you move on. For Mel, though, there were times that the supposedly clandestine monitoring was irritating. He was a grown man who knew more about some of the things on this ranch than she did. And he was always working alongside her right hand man whom she trusted, so what was with the micro-managing and watching? He occasionally joked to Lester when they knew she was watching that he was going to drop his pants around his ankles and jump around, pretending to swat at a non-existent bee. Lester never believed that he would do it, but always chuckled while cautioning him not to. Part of it was that Mel knew Terri to be somewhere near his own age, possibly even younger. So for her to persistently watch them like they were little boys bent on mischief without mommy to keep them straight annoyed him occasionally.

Still, the team was doing well, making headway, establishing patterns of task priorities. Terri's persistence with prospective customers was paying off with contracts that were growing longer in duration and a little more lucrative to boot. There was reason for cautious optimism that she might be able to make a go of it. Imagine, her, out here in this glorious, open setting, owning and operating a ranch where no one knew her. No shadows to pop out of her past, not a single reminder of the fake glitter and false promises that wrecked her, literally. People out here were real, focused on the important things in life; earning an honest living, helping their neighbors, raising a

34

family. That last one would never come her way, she knew, but she was fine with it. She could happily live out her years in this bucolic setting without knowing the blessings of motherhood. It was a perfectly fine trade off to the alternative otherwise known as her past.

The first year was a series of unrelenting disasters, nearly depleting her of financial reserves and the will to persevere. Slowly, she had learned to trust Lester and occasionally follow his advice. The irony was that Weaverly, the man from whom she'd bought the place, only gave her Lester's number as an afterthought as he was handing her the keys to the place. What if he hadn't? And what if she hadn't called him, as she almost didn't? Well, she wouldn't have lasted into her second year out here, that much was certain. With constant encouragement from the elder man, however, she learned some of the ropes. And when she failed, he sometimes made calls to old friends who owed him favors. And they never let him down. She wondered sometimes, over the years how many people had he helped? How many and how often, that all he had to do was pick up a phone and his request was met? He was not a man of any wealth or authority, but you'd have thought he was, given the way people regarded him. How often she had been in the grocery store or the feed store or church (the few times she talked herself into going) and was told by the people she met that she was so lucky to have Lester working for her? Now things were just starting to turn. She'd stopped losing money five months ago, broke even the next three and then actually made a tiny little bit of money the last two. Her forecast for the coming month was even better; she was probably going to be able to pay all her suppliers in the same month with a little bit left over. That was a first, and hopefully the first of more to come.

The two men went about their tasks each day, resting only for lunch that she made and set out for them. They would sit in the shade of her covered porch and discuss the varying degrees of success or failure of their morning's efforts and whether or not they needed to alter the plans they had concocted that morning. They very often did tweak their plans a little, usually placing the most physically difficult tasks immediately after lunch when they'd be rested and before the real heat of the day kicked in. The tasks for the hottest part of the day were arranged so they were something that could be done in the shade or at a slower pace. And they almost always took a little break under the awning of Mel's trailer for some iced tea in the afternoon. He sure liked his iced tea, and he'd gotten Lester hooked on it too. Not even two weeks had gone by before Lester got in the habit of "needing" his iced tea around 3PM. Yet even as they sat, they still discussed and planned their work to finish out the day. These two were all about their work, Terri observed, and knowing that was a huge relief.

This particular day drew to a close and she heard Lester's old Dodge pickup start up and roll past the house. She looked at the clock and knew it was time to get ready to drive over to the 4H meeting in Hulett. Out of boredom last winter, she decided to answer an ad seeking a volunteer to help run the local girls' 4H club. Turned out to be one of the best decisions she'd ever made. The engagement with the fresh faced young girls who were so full of life and optimism helped re-kindle a little bit of the girl she had lost. How often the room erupted into spontaneous laughter and she got swept up in it, laughing until she cried and slowly building camaraderie with those young ladies. She grabbed her purse, car keys and the large bag full of the art supplies she was going to need for the evening's project, and headed out the door. She saw Mel sitting at the little table under the trailer's awning, evidently enjoying another iced tea, and gave him a wave. He returned it, but without a smile she noted. Not that she had given him one, but still.

I Ran to Alva

Secret Alpha

"OK, we'll be back in about an hour." Terri advised Mel. She and Lester climbed into Lester's aged Dodge pickup and headed out the driveway in a cloud of dust and engine smoke.

Mel gathered the tools he thought he'd need to cut the rusted section of the barn's broken water pipe and then join a new length of pipe in with threaded unions. He was measuring the pipe when a loud and lifted Chevy 4wd truck came flying up the driveway and created huge dust cloud. Great. Dylan Turner had arrived. Terri mentioned he'd be coming by to pick up a few bales of barley hay, but she'd said it would be much later. Mel was wishing it had been, so Terri could deal with him.

Mel deliberately didn't look as Dylan backed up to the barn opening, then stepped out of the lifted truck and walked in to locate the hay. Mel stayed focused on the pipe fitting at hand, but his mind wandered back to the first day in town. That first morning in Ruby's diner when Dylan had confronted and attempted to bully him. Mel had to back down, for the first time in his life. There was too much to lose. The reward for taking down such a hot head would have earned him, what? Nothing. A reputation in a small town, maybe a jail cell, and an appointment with a judge. And who knows what kind of information would be revealed in a legal proceeding?

Still, he chuckled as he eavesdropped on the circus taking place in the barn. It sounded like Dylan had slipped or fallen off the ladder and was cursing up a purple storm. The barley bales were taking the brunt of his ire as he threw them with all possible force into the truck bed. Well, if he can do all that, reasoned Mel, he couldn't have hurt himself too badly. He heard the tailgate slam shut and was happy that Dylan would be leaving. But not just yet…

"Hey, Hollywood," Dylan called out to him snidely. "Tell your lady boss to get a new step ladder. The fu**in' thing broke under me. She's lucky I don't sue her."

"I'll tell her." Mel answered without looking at him.

"I ain't shittin' around, Hollywood," Dylan persisted. "You better fu**in' tell her."

Mel set down the hack saw and began walking toward the barn, and toward Dylan. He walked slowly and calmly, never allowing his face or his posture to betray what he was feeling. As he got ever closer to Dylan, he could see him start to posture, expecting a confrontation and apparently was eager for it. As Mel walked just a few inches past Dylan, he said calmly, "Let me take a look at that step ladder." Dylan never turned his back to Mel, rotating in his direction as he walked past, but the expected ambush never came. Mel just walked on by.

Dylan began to sneer. What a chicken shit, he thought. It actually surprised him that he was so timid, but some men just don't have the heart to fight, resigned to the fact that they are not the big dog in the room. Dylan was the Alpha. He was always the Alpha and made sure everyone knew it.

As Mel knelt by the broken step ladder, he asked Dylan, "How much do you weigh?"

"What the f**k – I dunno, about 245 maybe…."

"Then this is your fault."

"What?! What the f**k are you talking about you dipshit?" He was quickly getting agitated.

"It's says right here," he pointed to the decal on the top step, "rated for a maximum of 200 pounds. You broke it and you're going to buy Terri a new one. You're going to the store right now to buy a new one."

Dylan laughed through clenched teeth and then screamed, "Or what?!?!? What the f**k do you think you're gonna do to ME you f**k-ing Hollywood sissy?!?!?"

Mel stood and replied, "You're going to do it. Or I'm going to put your face down on this floor and remove the money from your wallet." He knew that would do the trick. The trap was loaded.

In a rage, Dylan lunged. Mel adroitly ducked the outstretched arms and brought his knee up into Dylan's abdomen. The blow forcibly expelled all the air from his lungs and nearly lifted him off the ground. He fell in a crumpled heap, gasping and coughing, his face beet red as his lungs cried for air. Mel moved and stood just a few feet away and said nothing. As Dylan's abdominal muscles began to relax and he drew a few shallow breaths, his anger surged once again. He reasoned that Mel must have some martial arts experience, so charging him like that was a mistake. He'd get off the ground and do it smarter, but smart or otherwise, he was gonna beat this guy's ass. Bad.

He smiled at Mel as he stood. "OK, Hollywood that was a good one. Let's see what else you got."

Mel said nothing. He stood relaxed with his arms at his side and shrugged his shoulders. Dylan had his hands up in fighting posture and was cautiously approaching Mel, circling around.

Mel turned in response to keep Dylan directly in front of him. Suddenly Dylan let go a tremendous right hook, the force of which had previously broken a man's jaw. Mel ducked it and brought his own left fist hard into Dylan's now-exposed right side. Again, the air left Dylan's lungs in great quantity. He struggled to remain on his feet, but dropped to one knee after a few seconds.

Mel stepped a few feet away, cautious not to take his eyes off Dylan. He figured Dylan's last desperate move would be to bull rush and tackle him to the ground. He was giving up about 30 pounds to Dylan and knew that the bigger man was capable of doing damage if given the opportunity.

"You f**king bitch!" Dylan yelled through gasps. "You're dead! You're dead! You're f**king dead!" He moved as though he was trying to stand, but as soon as he got his feet under him, lunged at Mel with surprising speed. Mel was just barely able to side step the charge, having underestimated Dylan's quickness if not his technique. But he missed and was now completely off balance and so he landed belly down on the hay covered floor. Mel immediately dove on top of him, wedged his right forearm into the back of Dylan's neck, then grabbed his left arm in the crook of the elbow and hiked it up behind his back. With these holds and with Mel's body weight squarely on top of him, there was nothing Dylan could do. He flailed about for a half minute before getting winded and feeling the increasing pain in his shoulder.

At last he settled down, still mad as hell but confused. He had never been in this situation, had never even come close to being on the losing end of a fight, but three attacks had been effortlessly dodged by "Hollywood" who now had him hog-tied. Clearly, Hollywood had some experience at this. Adding to Dylan's confusion was that Hollywood was not beating on him. He could have been pummeling the back of his head, the side of his face or his ribs, but he did nothing.

"Get the f**k off me," Dylan blustered.

"No," Mel said calmly, "I'll get off when you've settled down. You're still in a fighting mood. If I let you up, you'll come at me again and then I'm gonna get pissed off and hurt you. And I don't wanna do that."

"I'm not......I'm cool, OK, I'm cool! MY shoulder hurts – I ain't gonna start no more shit. Let me up."

"What about the step ladder?"

"Yeah. OK, I'll go buy a f**king ladder. Let me up."

"If you take off and don't come back with one, I will find you and I will make sure there's an audience to see it. Understand?"

Dylan grunted "Yeah." Mel released his hold, stood quickly and moved a few feet away just in case Dylan changed his mind. He was slow to his feet, moving his left arm in large circles attempting to alleviate the soreness. He did not look at Mel. Rather, he walked slowly over to the broken step ladder, examined it for a few seconds and said, "I'll be right back." He climbed into the big Chevy, started it and rolled gingerly out the driveway.

Mel wondered if Dylan would indeed go get the new step ladder, or perhaps retrieve a weapon instead, bent on escalating the conflict. - a worrisome thought. So he went to his trailer and retrieved the 9mm pistol from under the coffee maker. He resumed work on the rusted out section of pipe with the 9mm resting close by in the tool box. He knew the hardware store was only a couple miles up the road, so if Dylan did merely as he was told, he should be back very soon, but if he was gone longer, then Mel knew to expect trouble.

To his relief, it was only a few minutes until he heard the moaning of the Chevy's oversize mud tires on the road, slowing for the approach to the driveway. As it pulled close to Mel, he reached his hand inside the tool box and let it come to rest on the pistol. Without shutting off the engine, Dylan got out and pulled the step ladder from the pick up. He walked over and placed it in front of Mel. "There ya go. Brand spankin' new."

Mel could see that he was unarmed and so removed his hand from the toolbox. "Thank you," he said doing his best to sound grateful.

"Yeah, OK," Dylan stammered. "It's actually….. uhhh a better one. It's rated for more weight."

"I appreciate that."

"Yeah, no sweat, "Dylan said and he turned to get into the truck, but he stopped. "Hey… I gotta know man…. How'd you learn to fight like that? I ain't never been beat, I mean not even close and you ain't even as big as me."

"Older brothers and they're both tougher than me," he said flatly.

"Mmmm, one hell of a family."

"I suppose."

"Yeah, well I gotta get this hay back to my place."

"Dylan...... what happened here.... No one needs to know. This was nobody's business but ours. I won't be talking about it in town. I'd prefer you didn't either, but it's up to you."

"I s'pose. Yeah, it's probably best just between us."

At that, he got into the Chevy and left. Mel hoped that Dylan wouldn't develop a sense of hurt pride in the coming hours and days and thus renew the conflict. He knew that the next time he was around him he would have to keep a very sharp eye for an ambush. A very sharp eye. Yet his gut told him that was probably not the case. He didn't seem agitated or bitter when he left. Almost seemed... respectful. Well, a beating can have that effect on a man.

Mel finished the pipe repair, checked it for leaks and then went to his trailer to make lunch. He was sitting under the outside awning and devouring the sandwich when Terri and Lester returned. She walked straight to the barn with a bag in her hand, but then stopped at the entrance.
"What's with this new step ladder?" She asked Mel.

"Dylan came by to get that hay, and he accidentally broke the old one. So he went to the store and bought a replacement."

Slack jawed, she asked incredulously, "Dylan? Replaced it? What?"

Mel just shrugged.

"Did you say anything to him? What did you say?"

"Nothing really, he told me he broke the step ladder and thought he should replace it because he was too heavy for it. So he went and bought a better one."

"What?" Terri was dumbfounded, so was Lester. They both looked at each other in disbelief. "That guy never accepts responsibility for anything."

"No he doesn't," added Lester "and I've known him since he was a boy." Lester didn't say anything, but he was suspicious. Mel's jeans had a small tear in one knee. Both knees and upper legs were dirty and his shirt looked a little dirtier than it should have been, considering he had only fixed a pipe. Still, there were no tell tale marks on Mel's face or hands, so Lester had nothing concrete to go on. Still he wondered…. He'd heard a passing story from a few weeks before involving Dylan backing down a stranger without a fight in Ruby's place, but he didn't know any specifics. Not like any story involving Dylan being a bully was somehow unique, though. He hadn't been in Ruby's for breakfast in quite a long time. Maybe he should pay a visit this weekend.

I Ran to Alva

Hidden Treasures

"Hey Lester, where's she goin'?" Mel asked, as he watched the little Toyota move out the driveway and down the road.

"Goin' to visit her uncle in Billings. She'll be back t'morra. Uncle's gettin' along in years so she goes now and then to check on him."

"Ohhhhhhhh," he smiled. "You wanna help me with something?"

He hadn't seen Mel smile that big in the short time he'd known him, so he was wondering what the young man was up to. Always the nosey gadabout, he replied, "Sure."

The two men worked for a few hours in the large shed to remove all the junk, old fencing, gates and such that accumulated over the span of 20+ years. They made three separate piles; things that could be used as is, things that needed repair and things that were just plain scrap. The latter was the largest pile, by far.

"What you have in mind here?" Lester asked.

"Chickens, "Mel replied. "Terri was saying that she wants to get a lot more chickens, because she's been getting requests for more eggs from that big market down by Gillette. So I thought I'd clear the shed, build a new wall and door about 6 feet in from the back wall and then punch a small hatch into the back wall for the chickens to come and go. Should hold at least 60 and I could build it practically for free."

"Hey that ain't a half bad idea," the elder man affirmed.

At the very back of the shed, in its darkest and deepest shadows, something large sat under a canvas and a thick layer of dust. Something even Lester didn't know was there. The two men grabbed the canvas and pulled it forward.

"A tractor?" Lester laughed. "How the hell did a tractor get in here?"

"You didn't know?" Mel asked.

"No I had no idea. I ain't never really dug around in here before. I bet miss Terri don't know about it neither."

Mel had always held a fondness for tractors going back to the summers he worked on his grandfather's farm in Oklahoma. His grandpa was not only a great farmer, but had a real knack for working on the tractors, trucks and various machines. Over time, he'd taught Mel everything from changing tires to rebuilding engines. Mel enjoyed working on vehicles of all types, but especially tractors, owing to a bit of nostalgia of the days on grandpa's farm.

"Look at that," Mel observed,"Only one tire is flat. The rest are all holding air. Where's my compressor?"

"What for? You gonna air up the tire, then what?"

"Then you and I are gonna roll this old 8N out into the sunlight and give her a proper inspection."

"It's a 2N, ain't it?" Lester challenged.

"No, look at the fenders." Mel countered.

"Yep, it sho' enough is. You know your old Ford tractors."

"My grandpa had a few of them."

"Oh yeah, well go on and get that compressor and we'll see which of the three piles this thing belongs in," he chuckled.

Mel retrieved the compressor, filled the tire and listened intently for an air leak. He heard nothing, so he set about topping off the other tires as well. When they were of normal pressure, he reached up to the gear shifter and wiggled it a little until he found neutral. The two men rolled the little tractor out of the shed where it had undoubtedly sat through three presidential administrations.

At first blush, Mel could see that it was not missing any parts, a big plus. Even the 3-point hitch on the back was intact. So he hooked up a hose to a water bib and rinsed the old tractor off to get a better look. The gray and red paint were in surprisingly good condition. The wiring and hoses on the engine were all present, though some were obviously aged and in need of replacement. Even if the tractor couldn't be made to run for cheap, at least it would be worth a few hundred bucks to someone who would want to make it run. Terri would be happy about that.

"Whatcha gonna do now, mister tractor mechanic?" Lester asked playfully.

"Look for obvious reasons someone would have parked it. Something bad. Oil in the water. Water in the oil. Metal in the oil. Blown gaskets. Stuff like that." Mel pulled the oil dipstick and saw that the oil was obviously old and dirty, but no evidence of water. Likewise, he turned the coolant drain valve and watched the aged, dirty water pour out. A little rust, but no oil. Very encouraging. At this point, it was worth looking at the fuel system and maybe hooking a battery up to see it if it would turn over.

He retrieved a screwdriver and a large bucket and then disconnected the fuel line from the carburetor. He moved the bucket under the open end of the fuel line and opened the fuel valve. The liquid that flowed out may have been gasoline at one time, but now was a thick, smelly goop that resembled maple syrup and napalm. Lester crinkled his nose and took a couple steps back, chuckling.

"Guess that gas tank will need some rinsing, "Mel observed.

"Ya think?" Lester laughed.

About a gallon of the petroleum-based goop drained into the bucket before it stopped. Mel made a note to buy some kerosene to pour into the tank as a rinsing agent. And if the fuel tank was that gummed up, the carburetor had to be a whole new level of nasty. He would look at that later. Next was to see if the old girl would even crank over and if the cylinders had any compression. He'd need his generator for that.

The two men rolled the old 8N next to his trailer because the built-in generator had a 12 volt outlet with cables that Mel could hook directly to the tractor's certainly-dead battery. Mel opened the battery hatch, saw the battery and suddenly remembered these old Fords had 6 volt electrical systems. He reasoned that brief hits of 12 volts shouldn't do any damage to the starter. He remembered his grandpa jumping the old tractors many times with the farm trucks that had regular 12 volt electrical systems.

He fired up the generator, attached the cables and jokingly yelled "fire in the hole!" at Lester before turning the key. To his delight, the little 4-cylinder engine rotated quite easily with no undue clanking, groaning, scraping or other fatal sounds. So it was time for a compression check.

He removed all four spark plugs and then attached the compression test gauge to the first cylinder. He had Lester turn the key while he held the gauge to watch the reading. It was a tad low at 80 pounds per square inch (psi), but not bad considering how long it had been since the engine had run. They repeated the sequence for each of the other 3 cylinders and both were surprised that all 4 hovered right around 80 psi. A very good sign. This engine had some life left in her.

All that remained was to check for spark, so Mel put one spark plug back into its respective wire cap and let it rest against the engine block to complete the circuit. He had Lester turn the key again and was surprised to see the bright white arc jump across the spark plug's electrode. So all that remained was to remove and inspect the carburetor and flush the fuel tank. He was optimistic. He had the carburetor off in 10 minutes.

"I'm going into town for some oil and new spark plugs for this little gal," he told Lester. "Can you think of anything else?"

"Air filter might be a good idea," Lester offered.

"Oh yeah! And kerosene to flush the fuel tank. Can't forget that. Maybe a fuel filter too, just in case."

"And some new fuel lines. Why chance those old ones?"

"Good idea."

A few minutes later, Mel jumped into the big crew cab and headed to the auto parts store. Lester was sitting on the porch enjoying his pipe when Mel returned an hour later. He walked over to see if Mel needed help carrying anything.

"How'd it go? Didja find everything?"

"Sure did – including some Berryman's for dipping the carburetor body when I tear it down. I also took a chance and bought a new battery"

"Mmmmm, well, looks like you got it covered."

"Yeah, something to do for the evening."

"Ha, not me, I'm goin' home. You have fun young man."

Mel tore apart the simple carburetor in just a few minutes and placed all the pieces into the dip basket for an overnight soak. Then he put the 5 gallons of kerosene into the tractor's fuel tank, also to soak overnight. In another hour or so, he had changed its oil, coolant, fuel lines and spark plugs. That's enough for one day's work, he thought, and should be more than adequate to bring her to life after being dormant so long.

He cleaned up, made a simple dinner and then sat outside to eat and to enjoy the setting sun. One thing he'd have to get used to was how quickly it cooled down around here after the sun went down. The bugs were soon flitting all around the lights under the awning and a few of them made low altitude passes over his head, so he decided it was time to go in. Not quite time for bed, so he fired up his laptop for a little 'net surfing and to catch up on some news.

One of Mel's favorite 'net pastimes was perusing maps of various areas. He spent more than an hour looking at the area around Alva, Hulett, Spearfish and a dozen other little hamlets. He even looked at the route Terri would have taken to go to Billings. To his surprise, it wasn't really all that far, but not being from the area, it just sounded far because she was "going to Montana."

After a while, he started to wonder if anything was being said about him. So he typed his name into Google and looked at about 5 pages of returns. Nothing new. Good. Ditto for Bing. Not like he was a major celebrity or anything, but he wondered if anyone would pay attention to his sudden absence, especially anyone in the sporting media. He just wanted them all to go away. He put all of it behind him in one big dramatic move and hoped everyone would forget him.

So far, this place was reminding him a little of his grandpa's old farm in Oklahoma. People moved at about the same pace, seemed to have about the same values. If his grandpa hadn't died and the family not agreed to sell the farm, that's where he would have gone. Without that option, there were no obvious choices for an escape. Funny how just a few months ago he was all mired in to the rat race otherwise known as Los Angeles, but with the magic of the internet, he'd found this job, in this place, with these people who knew nothing and he hoped would ask nothing. And if not for those summers on grandpa's farm, he'd have never acquired the skills necessary to be here in the first place. What would he have done? There was no guarantee that this place and this job were even going to work out in the long haul, he knew that, but it was what he needed now. How fortunate he felt that everything had lined up when it did. With that little bit of peace in his heart, he went to bed.

He awoke about a half hour before the sunrise, no alarm needed, as he had always been an early riser. He hit the start button on the coffee maker that he'd loaded the night before and proceeded to choose the work clothes for the day at hand. He found the oldest and most worn out items he had and put them on, as he was anticipating getting greasy, not just dirty, working on the tractor. While drinking his first cup of coffee, he made a list of things to check on the tractor, presuming it did start and run after he put some fresh gas in it and got the carburetor back on.

He was kind of excited at the prospect of getting the tractor going. To him, machines had their own persona and their own character and he often wondered if the machine performed better for you out of gratitude when you kept it maintained and clean. In that train of thought, how grateful then would the old 8N be to the man who saved her from that dark, dank shed after more than two decades and brought her back to life? He hoped she would run well, just on a practical level, because there were several things Terri wanted done around the place that required a tractor and she was dreading the rental fees. The little Ford didn't have a front end loader bucket, but the PTO on the back would power the implements necessary to do most of anything that needed doing – if it worked.

After breakfast, he retrieved the dip bucket of Berryman's and removed the carburetor body and parts from the basket inside. He then gave them a quick soaking rinse in a bucket of hot water and then a blast from the nozzle off the air compressor to dry everything out. The sun was up now, so he held each piece up in its direction to be certain light was coming through the portals and passages that needed to be clear. All looked good. Reassembly on such a simple little carburetor only took a few minutes and he had it bolted back on.

Mel then drained the kerosene from the tractor's fuel tank back into the 5-gallon container. He was relieved to see that only the first couple gallons came out murky, and then cleared up nicely and with no rust. He put on a new fuel line and then put a couple gallons of gas in the tank. He turned on the fuel valve and waited a few seconds for it to fill the carburetor bowl before trying the starter. "Well, here goes nothing," he muttered as he turned the key.

The little engine turned obediently, but did not fire. He pulled the choke lever out about half way and cranked it a few seconds. No fire. He pulled the choke lever all the way to the stop and cranked a few seconds more. Still no fire. Hmmmm…. He got down out of the seat and checked the carburetor bowl drain to see if fuel was present. It was, so why didn't the engine…. and then he saw the loose coil wire. "Rookie," he chastened himself as he had forgotten to reconnect the coil after the previous day's testing. The unconnected wire meant no spark. He stuck it on the connector and got back up in the seat. A quick turn of the key and the little engine jumped to life.

"Ha HAAAAAAAA!!!!!!!!!!!" he shouted with delight, but then looked around to be sure no one had been watching him.

For the next ten minutes, he let the little engine run while he inspected for oil leaks, water leaks, fuel leaks, overheating, anything that he had not yet encountered, but even the charging system was working fine, as the ammeter told him. Time for a test ride, maybe there was something wrong in the clutch, transmission or axles.

One nice thing about living in a rural community was no one thought twice about running a tractor down the local highways, so Mel pointed the little Ford out the driveway to the road for a shake down run. She moved easily through all four gears and Mel was content to let her run along at roughly 20 mph. The oil pressure and temperature gauges were rock steady and nothing was leaking, Mel was excited. After a couple minutes, he throttled back, applied the brakes and moved to the shoulder of the road. The brakes worked well enough to lock the wheels in the soft gravel when he really stomped on the pedal. That was a pleasant surprise, because the N-series Fords weren't well renowned for their brakes. He checked for traffic and pulled back onto the road to head for home.

He was about halfway back when a rusty old Dodge Power Wagon truck passed him cautiously. It was Lester, and the look on his face was priceless. Pure shock and disbelief. He was already out of his truck when Mel rolled the little tractor in the driveway and stopped next to him.

"Well, I'll be damned!" he exclaimed "You really got it runnin'! And it runs good too! You done good! Real good! Listen to it purr!"

Mel was pleased at Lester's reaction. The first couple days of the two working together was a bit uneasy because of so many differences between them and so little in common. Mel had had to win Lester over through his work ethic and ability to do "farm stuff." He knew from the start that Lester would be reporting back to Terri on whether or not it was going to work out, and he knew that Terri would listen. Impressing Lester would indirectly impress Terri, and he'd get to stay. For sure he didn't need the job for the money, but he needed it for the space, the time and opportunity it gave him to 'be somewhere" without being anywhere. Anywhere people would know him, that is.

"Man, miss Terri is sure gonna be surprised!" Lester said with a big smile.

"Yeah, and you and I won't have to dig those post holes by hand to fix that fence by the creek. We can rent a PTO digger to mount on the back of this little gal for only about $30 a day. Piece of cake." Mel beamed.

"Yeah, hey, speaking of money," Lester began, "how much did you spend getting this ol' girl going?"

"Maybe 90 bucks – why?"

"Well, don't expect that Miss Terri can pay you back all at once. I think she's on a pretty tight string."

"That's not a problem. I'm in no hurry for it."

"Yeah.... You seem sorta.... well-heeled for a travelin' ranch hand. Ain't too many folk aroun' here got a truck and trailer rig like yours. No sir, that's some nice rig you got goin' down the road there."

Mel smiled, "What do you want to know, Lester?"

"Well," the older man hesitated, "you can't blame a fella for being curious about someone he ain't never met before. I mean you come all the way from Los Angeles to take this job for ten bucks an hour and show up in a rig that none of us can afford. It makes a fella wonder."

"Fair enough...," he paused and drew a breath, "Until a few months ago, I was a professional athlete," He began, careful to leave out certain details, "and I lived in LA. I saw a lot of guys get hurt and it never bothered me until I was the one who hurt someone. So I left. I never lived a flashy life style, so I saved a lot of the money I made and that's how I can afford the rig. I ain't ever going back, even if I leave here someday. So I am on the run, Lester. Not from the law, but from myself and who I was. If I spend the rest of my life making ten bucks an hour so that I never have to feel that way again, it'll be a happy life. And I would very much appreciate you not repeating this. It's my business and I hope you can respect that."

The older man was somber, caught off guard by the sincerity and depth of the answer. "Yeah, hell yeah, no I won't say nothin'. We all carry things, though. All of us. We all done things we wish we hadn't. Don't carry it too long though, son, it'll keep you from doin' stuff you should be doin'. Let it go sometime."

"I'll try to remember that."

"Allright then," he smiled at Mel. "What's say we load all that scrap metal into the trailer and turn it in at the scrap yard? I reckon we got a couple hunnert bucks worth."

"Let's do it," Mel affirmed, "only don't you even *think* about putting this little gal in that scrap trailer, "Mel said as he patted the little tractor's fender.

"Oh no no…"he said, holding up his hands, "that there is one of them things you stumble across only a time or two in your life. That there's a treasure and we done dug it up. I tell you what – Miss Terri is gonna be just plum pleased."

I Ran to Alva

Less than Gracious

Lester walked over to Mel's trailer, where he was sitting under the awning enjoying an iced tea. "Miss Terri expects to be home in about an hour. I just spoke with her on the phone."

"Oh good, I can't wait to see her face when she realizes she owns a working tractor."

Lester chuckled. "Yeah, that'll be a good one. And that we cleaned out that shed. Then we'll hand her the $180 cash we got for the scrap metal. Should be a good home comin."

"Yep. Hey, you want some tea?"

"Don't mind if I do. You gettin' me hooked on it."

The two men sat and discussed the various projects needed and what their priorities should be and how the tractor could be used to their benefit. Before long, Lester began concocting a way to make the tractor a big surprise for Terri.

"We can't just have it sittin' next to the barn and say "there it is"", he opined. "We gotta do somethin'."

"What did you have in mind, something sneaky?" Mel said, grinning.

"Natcherly."

After some discussion, they decided to park it in the newly cleared shed. They plotted to coax her over to look at the shed and ask what she thought the space could be used for. Then they hoped to see her face light up when she saw it and rehearsed their explanation on how the tractor came to be.

"Yep, that's a great plan," Mel affirmed. They backed the little Ford just far enough into the shed so that it couldn't be seen from the driveway. As the time approached for her return, the two men, young and old, grew giddy with anticipation. At long last, her Toyota pulled into the drive and next to the house. They walked casually over to greet her.

"Heyyyyyyy Miss Terri," Lester greeted her warmly, "glad you're back safe and sound," he said with a big smile. Mel nodded and smiled in agreement.

"Thank you Lester," she said coldly, "it was a long drive and I'm tired."

Her mood and attitude caught both men quite off guard, but Lester was not deterred.

"Well, we done some things while you was gone that might cheer you up."

"Maybe so, Lester, but right now I'm looking at that old, beat up utility trailer sitting in front of the barn and you know I want it parked out back so I don't have to look at it."

"Yes ma'am, well we used it to.."

"I can see that you used it," she cut him off. "I can also see that you did not put it back where it belongs."

Mel let out a long, loud exhale and walked away. "What crawled up her butt?" he muttered under his breath. And Lester seemed a little slow on the uptake, but he saw that Mel had walked away and decided to follow him. Mel had not seen this side of Terri before and did not like it in the least. Best to step away for now. She made no attempt to talk to either of them or to follow them toward Mel's trailer, but went inside the house. Lester pulled the folded money out of his shirt pocket and handed it to Mel.

"Screw this," he said with resignation. "You give it to her. And when she decides she can treat me decent, then have her call me and I'll come back to work. Guess I'll see ya whenever." He walked to the old Dodge truck, got in and drove away.

Mel was stunned. Lester had basically quit, unless and until Terri decided she owed him an apology, and she didn't seem the apologetic type. This could be bad. He'd grown to like Lester and looked forward to working with him each day. Something was obviously bothering her, but was this the shape of things to come? Was she always this moody and bitchy? Maybe she had a right to be in this instance, maybe she'd gotten some really bad news while she was gone, or maybe it was trivial and overblown. It was his first real glimpse at her personality, as she had thus far been a closed book, and he didn't like what he saw.

He went inside the trailer and got a cold bottle of stout from the refrigerator and went back outside and sat under the awning. He placed the money on the table and then set his folding Buck knife on it so the breeze wouldn't blow it away. He nursed the stout very slowly, the way he enjoyed it best. By the time he'd gotten half way through it, the sun was setting and he began to relax, but realized he hadn't eaten dinner, so he stepped into the trailer to scrounge something up. In the fridge, he spotted the leftover pasta and sausage from the previous night and it looked as good as anything else, so he threw it in the microwave and sat down at the dinette to eat. He had already learned the hard way not to eat outside after sundown, as the awning lights attracted every sort of flying bug in the county and none of them were shy about helping themselves to his dinner.

He finished eating, then put the dishes into the RV's diminutive dishwasher and opened another stout. He deliberated whether to go back outside and sit or to fire up the computer and surf the 'Net. He opted for the latter and was just getting started when there was a knock on his door.

"Just a minute," he said, knowing it was Terri and being sure to let her hear the unreceptive tone in his voice. He opened the door and stepped away without saying a word. She walked in, obviously feeling a little tense and Mel could sense that she was not sure how to start the conversation. Hell, maybe she was gonna tell him to pack up and go. He really didn't care. He didn't even look at her.

"When I came home earlier..." she hesitated, "I was...."

"Less than gracious." He finished the sentence, as he turned to look her square in the eye.

She looked at the floor and continued, "You're right, I was. I was rude to both of you. I'm sorry, and sorry to Lester, too."

"You'll have to call him and tell him yourself. He basically....left your employment.... Until he feels that he's welcome back here."

"You're kidding!" she replied in shock.

"Not in the least. He's worked for you for how long now? Ever since you bought the place, right? Taught you damn near everything you need to know about living out here. Men like that don't take kindly to being insulted. But you call him. I'm sure he'll accept your apology and come back. He seems reasonable enough."

"I will… I never meant to insult him. I need him here. I really do."

Mel just shrugged his shoulders, "Well, he doesn't feel that way right now, I can tell you that."

She let out a long sigh and looked at the floor again. She turned to leave, but then said, "You left some money out on the table."

"That's yours."

"Mine? How is it mine?"

"You'd know that if you hadn't been so rude."

"Ummm, OK, yeah…… I had that coming. But…"

"We thought we'd surprise you. We cleaned out that shed so I could build a new chicken coop at the back. There was a lot of scrap metal in there, so we loaded it into the utility trailer. You know the trailer we carelessly left in front of the barn? Anyway, we took it all to the scrap yard. We got about $180 for it. That's your money. "

"Oh, uhhhhh….that is a nice surprise. I….ummmm….wasn't expecting that." She immediately began wondering why neither he nor Lester had conspired to *keep* the money. She had no idea that scrap metal would be worth anything and they probably knew she wouldn't know. They could have told her they just hauled it away and she'd have been none the wiser. She'd have been happy simply to have the shed cleared out. That was a nice thing to know about both the men, Mel especially.

"There's one more thing," Mel continued. "We didn't throw away everything we found in the shed.'

"Like what?"

"Go look," he instructed.

She stepped out of the trailer, hoping he was going to follow, but he didn't. So she continued alone to the shed, uncertain of what she was going to find, yet she knew it had to be something good, given that the men had kept it. When she got to the shed opening, she flipped the light switch and could hardly believe her eyes. A tractor! She had no idea what kind it was, she didn't know a thing about it, but she knew one thing: that Lester had been telling her all along to save her money for a tractor. With a tractor, he said, all the things that need to be done around a place like this can be done three times as fast and with three times less effort.

She walked around it, trying to read anything she could to learn about it. She saw the levers and controls up by the driver's seat, but had no idea what any of them did. She bumped her shin on the 3-point hitch frame as she walked around the rear, but was so enamored by the contraption that she didn't even say "Ow." The gray and red paint was kinda neat and old-timey. She wondered if it ran. If not, would it be worth fixing it up? She found herself amused at the notion that the tractor was rather "cute." Not a big, scary, earth shaking monster, but certainly not a dinky little riding mower. It was perfect.

"Start it," Mel said, standing in the opening. She was startled, as she hadn't heard him walk up.

"It runs?" she asked excitedly.

"Runs great," he affirmed. "She didn't run when we found her, but only needed a couple parts and some TLC."

"I didn't know you could fix tractors," she replied.

"Then you didn't read my emails closely enough," he said, feigning a look of disapproval. "Start it," he said again, "I'll show you how. It's almost the same as a car."

He showed her the ritual of the fuel valve, the throttle and the choke and gave a brief explanation on the why's of each. He noted by the questions she asked that she understood right away. "Now turn the key," he instructed.

The little engine started immediately, belching black smoke until she remembered to push off the choke as he had instructed. "WoooooHOOOO!" she screamed and Mel could only smirk at her reaction. She was fist pumping in the air and bouncing in the seat. "It's awesome!" she screamed.

Mel felt his mood lift as he watched her celebrate like a 6 year old on Christmas morning, but he squelched his smile rather quickly, unsure if her jubilation was just the other side of the mood swing coin. He'd be sure to observe her a little more carefully before he opened up any more.

"I want to drive it. Right now," she said with a huge smile.

"Not tonight, the lights don't work. I had to order headlight bulbs; they'll be in in a couple of days. You can drive her tomorrow."
"Ohhhhh all right," she said with obvious disappointment in her voice. She turned the engine off and then sat and admired the little tractor for a moment before getting out of the seat.

"Fuel valve," Mel instructed. "Every time. Turn it off every time."

"Oh yeah," she located the knob and obediently turned it off, patting the little tractor's hood as she did so. "We're going to be good friends."

She proceeded to ask Mel every single little detail about how he and Lester found the tractor, what he did to get it running and what he thought its capabilities were around the farm. They stood and talked for about 20 minutes, during which she asked him twice about the parts he'd bought. When he dodged the question for the third time, she came straight to the point.

"Exactly how much money did you spend on the tractor?"

"I don't know, I'd have to look at the receipts. It was maybe fifty bucks or something."

"Bull. You said you bought a battery. That alone is more than fifty bucks."

He was surprised she knew that. "OK, OK, geeeezzzz, it's not that big a deal. I'm pretty sure the total was right around a hundred and ten, I can tell you for sure tomorrow."

She counted $120 out of the scrap money and held it out for Mel to take. He hesitated, so she stuffed it into his shirt pocket as he stood awkwardly. "If it's less than that, you can give me the change tomorrow. Mel, I have a good impression of you, but we are not friends. Well, not yet anyway. You are my employee and our relationship is based on business and work. If you spend money for my benefit, then it should be settled right away. Understood?"

"Sure," he said. He was not accustomed to women being so matter of fact and direct. Then again, he did get that impression from her first emails. She had asked a lot of questions and didn't make any chit-chat. That was good, he reasoned. Maybe he could believe her if he asked her how she was and she replied "fine."

Standing this close to her, he realized that she was actually quite pretty. He hadn't been within arm's reach of her before and she was not the type to stand still and make eye contact. He hadn't previously been able her observe her face for this long. She didn't exactly do anything to attract a man's attention; that was clear. She was never made up, never wore anything but loose fitting jeans and shirts and generally wore boots.

Something in his eyes told her that he was seeing her….as a woman… and she immediately felt uncomfortable. "And so what about the labor charges to get her running? Anything extra there?"

Mel was caught a little off guard. The three seconds they'd spent looking at each other in close proximity had erased the conversation from his mind. "What? Oh no, Terri, I worked on it basically on "your time" that you already pay me for. There are no extra charges."

"OK, well, thank you. I am grateful. I will call Lester…. maybe even right now….and throw myself at his feet I guess."

"No, don't go over the top. Lester's a simple man who just wants to be treated fairly. Just tell him you had a bad day and acted rudely and you're sorry. That's all a man needs really in an apology. Keep it simple."

"Simple?"

"Yeah, simple."

"OK…… Uhhhh, Mel?"

"Yeah."

"I had a bad day, got some bad news about my uncle, but it wasn't right to be rude to you and I'm sorry."

It was funny how he hadn't seen it coming and funnier still that he was so speechless. Her soft, sincere apology took him completely off balance. His stammering and clumsy response, "Well…….ummmm….I'm sorry about your uncle…..OK……..ummmmmm….I hope he improves……I guess we're…..good."

She laughed to herself at his inarticulate reply and understood with her woman's intuition that they were on even ground again, which pleased her.

"I will see you in the morning then?"

"Yep."

He turned and walked toward the trailer and she toward the house. He was about halfway there when he turned back to look at her, not really knowing why. She had stopped by the rose bush at the base of the front porch steps and was fiddling with it for some reason. All he could really see of her was a silhouette, backlit as she was by the bright halogen porch light, but the silhouette was…. A woman…. with a striking figure. He couldn't process it. It was the same woman? How…

"Is there something else Mel?" she called to him.

"B-uhhhhh no, nothing. I was just….I'll see you tomorrow."
And he made haste toward the trailer.

That was odd, she thought.

I Ran to Alva

Rebuilding the Team

The next morning, Mel awoke at his customary 5am, got the coffee maker going and psyched himself up for the workout. Not easy to do after a night of uneasy thoughts and interrupted sleep. He still bristled when he thought of Terri's cold attitude toward him and Lester when she came home. Sure she had apologized, sincerely, and he believed and accepted it, but he wondered how she would approach Lester and what she would say. And how would Lester react? He was pretty cheesed off when he left last night. No doubt Mel would be working on his own today as it would probably take most of the day for Lester to cool off after talking to her, and he'd take the day off just to make the point.

He was also pre-occupied at the thought or the question about her personality, overall. The woman who came home all cold and bitchy was not the same woman whom he saw so delighted, even giddy, sitting atop the little tractor. Which one was Terri? He was having a difficult time wrestling with the issue. It shouldn't matter at all and it wouldn't have, except for the three seconds they stood in the shed, close together, and he saw her eyes for the first time, really saw them. They seemed to belong to a woman who was soft and sentimental, not distant and guarded. He felt for a brief moment like he had really looked at her, and then she turned away so awkwardly. What had she seen in his eyes that she didn't like? Damn, that was a thought and not a pleasant one to contemplate. Maybe she saw inside him, too, and maybe she saw that guy he was running from. Was that even possible? Couldn't be, because that guy was not really Mel. He was a caricature, someone fabricated out of whole cloth to generate "buzz" to create a name, a mystique. That wasn't really him though. She could not have seen that guy because he doesn't exist. So what did she see then, that made her move away? And then it occurred to him, maybe what she saw was his sentiment. He knew at the moment it happened that he was surprised to be drawn to her eyes and when he made contact, was essentially unable to look away. Did she see that? If so, then why was that a problem? He answered that question for himself; it was a problem on a thousand different fronts. Not the least of which was the fact that he worked for her and they were basically strangers. Still, his gut told him he had in fact answered the question. She'd seen the curiosity in his eyes when he looked into hers and she felt vulnerable.

It was only because of those three seconds that the question of her personality even mattered. If not for those three seconds, he'd have written her off merely as some kind of a fickle, temperamental woman not to be given another thought. Do the work and collect the paycheck, ignore the mood swings. If not for those three seconds. And it was all that tangled mess that kept him awake last night. He thought about going back to bed now and getting some more sleep, but it was never a serious thought, with the way he was raised and his own internal work ethic.

So he threw on some comfortable sweats and his favorite training shoes and headed to the rear of the trailer – the garage-where the all-in-one workout station awaited his arrival. He went through his customary 45 minute workout, showered and sat down to consider what he was going to do today. On a normal day, he'd expect to hear Lester's noisy old Dodge come plodding up the driveway any minute now and he'd greet him outside with a cup of coffee and they would sit and plan the day based on Terri's list. Oh! The list. He headed out the door and walked over to the front porch of her house to retrieve the list she always set on the flat top of the lowest rail post. To his surprise, it was not there. Well, that was all right; there were still a couple unfinished things from yesterday that he knew they would have tackled anyway. So he figured he would start in on those at least until he saw Terri up and about when he could ask her. He walked back to his trailer and was preparing to gather his work gloves when he heard the familiar rumbling and creaking of the Dodge. A smile crossed his face and he turned to look out the window. He quickly poured two cups of coffee and headed out the door. Lester received the coffee with gratitude and they sat at the little table to discuss the day.

"Wasn't sure I'd see you today." Mel commented.

"Yeah….well…Miss Terri called me up last night and we talked it out. It's good, but she is a high strung filly, that one. Worries over every tiny little thing, worries too much. Way too much. She was awf'ly grateful over the tractor though. Called you a wizard."

"She did not."

"Did so, called you a wizard, she did. She likes you. Didn't say that, but I been around. I know."

"You don't know half what you think you know old man," Mel said, teasing.

71

"I know twice what you think I know, you young pup," he replied with a broad smile.

"Uh-huh…well, all that aside, she didn't leave us a list, so we'll have to go on what we left from yesterday until we can talk to her.'

"Nope. Said there won't be no more lists. Said we gon' talk every day, all of us, face to face. Said we's a team that needs to work together."

Mel was stunned. "That's weird. I mean, I'm glad she won't look down her nose at us, but… I hope she doesn't start telling us *how* to do what we're supposed to do."

Lester laughed. "You read my mind, young pup. You're smarter than you look. I said that very thing to her on the phone last night. Just tell me what you want done. Don't tell me how to do it unless you have more 'sperience at it than I do. She agreed. She ain't really gonna tell us nothin', just said she wants to hear more from us about what we do, what slows us down, what could she do for us?"

"Wait – she said all that?"

"Yeah. Hey listen now… people sometimes need a little confrontation like what happened last night to wake up and change. People can change, but sometimes they need time and mebbe an event to let them know they need to change. It don't never occur to nobody to change, all on they own. Nobody thinks that way. We all think we perfect in our own little ways and we ain't inclined to change no way, until somethin' happens, tells us we need to."

Mel slumped back in his chair. "Yeah, I totally get that."

Lester observed the younger man for a couple seconds. "Well, allright then. Maybe you had one of them events. Maybe you responded to it the right way. Maybe you should allow that Miss Terri could do the same?'

"You're a lot smarter than *you* look," Mel deliberately echoed Lester's earlier comment. The two men smiled, sipped their coffee and sat quietly for a bit.

They were surprised when they saw Terri emerge from the house. She walked directly toward them, waving and smiling from the distance as she approached.

"You got any more coffee?" she asked Mel when she arrived.

"Uh… yeah, of course," he clumsily replied. Lester smiled without letting Mel see.

He went inside to pour it and called out, "How do you like it?"

"Straight up," she replied, which Mel interpreted as no cream or sugar. He smiled at the low maintenance, no frills, implication. He came back out, placed her cup on the table and retrieved another of the matching chairs that had thus far been folded up and stored out of the way, since he and Lester had made use of only two.

She took her place at the table and the three of them began discussing their successes and achievements, and what was yet to be done. She gave them a little insight as to the markets and grocery stores she'd been negotiating with, shared some of the horror stories of her interactions. Both men exchanged occasional nods and glances, knowing that she was uniquely suited to the work she was doing and they were grateful they didn't have to do it. Mel himself suddenly realized that what really made this place work, what really provided him and Lester with a paycheck, was Terri. For all her inexperience with crops, livestock, tractors, feed, soil and weather, she knew things about people, money, sales, and egos about which he and Lester were utterly clueless. He began to consider, to wonder, if they all depended on each other. The experience and the hard working efforts of he and Lester mattered nothing if there were no takers, no buyers, for the results of what they produced. And he also considered the idea that she might be the best marketer and sales person in the world, but would have to fold her tent if she could not produce. Those thoughts were not exclusively Mel's. The exchange and light hearted banter at the table had the same thoughts circling around in Lester's mind, and in Terri's. Together, they were beginning to achieve and they could continue to achieve, with an appreciation of what each brought to the table.

While Mel's gears were turning in this regard, so were Terri's. She was smart enough to know that in reality, she knew nothing about the challenges these men faced in doing their jobs. She knew nothing about how hard it was to dig a hole for a fence post, to pull a 1200 pound cow out of a stream bed without injuring it, to stack and load 600 eggs without breaking a single one. Her desire to live here, to remain here, to be happy here, was dependent on her own diligence, but also her ability to see and understand what the men did and to foster an understanding with them that she appreciated what they did. She could not be Marie Antoinette with any hope of a lasting, meaningful existence in this rough but beautiful country. She would have to bring them in, to let them in, to seek their counsel, but also take steps to make their jobs somehow less difficult.

As they sat and sipped at the coffee, Terri suddenly realized the value of the time that the two men always spent at the beginning of their days. There had been a few days she'd woken up early to the sound of Lester's truck, peered out at the two of them , young and old, sitting at the table, drinking coffee, looking at the list, exchanging laughter and gestures, and wondered what the hell they could possibly be accomplishing. Now she knew. They were "achieving" the most valuable thing of all; they were building trust, camaraderie, and a sense of commitment to each other. She really hoped, prayed, that she could join them on these mornings without them feeling like she was an intruder, and they would include her. Would these two hard working men be able to open up and accept her as a part of their morning coffee?

"Can we do this tomorrow, too?" she asked, looking uncertainly back and forth at Lester and Mel.

"I wouldn't have it any other way Miss Terri," Lester said.

She looked at Mel for affirmation. He deliberately did not answer, looking as he was into her eyes and knowing that she would break eye contact as soon as he gave it. He peered into her eyes without blinking, without deflection, for what she thought was an hour, yet she never looked away. And he considered as he looked. "Yeah," he replied as he stared, looking for hesitation, doubt or anything at all that might betray a sign of insincerity. Seeing none, he smiled just a little and then as he predicted, she did look away, but the message had been sent.

"Allright then," Lester replied, cutting the silence and barely able to contain a smile, "Let's get to work."

The dust up over the tractor and the misplaced utility trailer was soon put behind them and a new sense of team work emerged. Gone were the days of Terri leaving the task list out for the men to retrieve without a word spoken between them. The new routine was the three of them meeting for coffee outside Mel's trailer each morning; they rarely sat and talked for more than 20 minutes before setting about their daily plans. On the occasional rainy day, they'd meet inside Mel's trailer to be more comfortable. Lester and Terri were both impressed at how tidy he kept the place, given bachelors' slovenly reputations.

One rainy morning, Mel gave them the "50 cent tour." Lester was impressed by all the techy gadgets it contained, while Terri was more interested in the family pictures and mementos he had tastefully displayed. She didn't ask about any of them, however. They both teased Mel about the "garage" at the rear of the trailer, especially considering it had a workout station and that fancy carbon fiber road bicycle hanging upside down.

"Who travels with their gym equipment?" Lester laughed.

"Hey Lester, he's single. He's gotta stay in shape for the ladies," Terri joined in.

Mel enjoyed the banter, even at his expense.

"Or the men?" Lester joked.

"Hey!" Mel playfully smacked him on the shoulder, "You said you wouldn't tell."

Lester howled with laughter, but Terri just rolled her eyes and pretended not to be amused. "Boys," she said, disdainfully.

But she looked as much as she dared, at this or that picture or nic-nac, anything that told her something more about him; especially the pictures with him and other people. The one with the pretty blond girl caught her attention, "Who's this, Mel? She's pretty."

Lester had to look away so neither could see him smiling.

"My cousin Myra. That pic was taken right after she won the Oklahoma Barrel Racing championship. She's an amazing rider."

"That's very interesting," Terri replied.

The new pattern of morning coffee quickly became the preferred one. Terri took copious notes regarding things the men said were challenges to their tasks, especially if it involved the purchasing or renting some kind of specialty equipment. They all agreed that maintaining a tight budget was imperative, but she kept a wish list of things to buy, based on what the men told her was of highest priority. The little tractor was going to help a lot, but it didn't have any implements, or tools, so in and of itself was limited. They needed to add things like post hole diggers, loaders and the like to increase the tractor's viability. The men also learned to ask her about the errands she ran each day and, where possible, did them for her, the goal being to reduce the amount of time she spent doing menial tasks. This freed more time for her to make contacts, sales and handle issues with the customers or the suppliers. Their weeks became a well-oiled repetition of tasks that each understood. Friday nights, they sometimes got pizza and beer and enjoyed it on Terri's screened front porch. It was nice to sit out during the evenings and enjoy the cool outside air without constantly swatting at every flying insect known to man. Saturdays usually had some minor things that needed doing, simple repairs or cleaning of this or that, but nothing major. And Sundays each went their own separate ways. Terri usually headed out Saturday afternoons to see her uncle up in Billings and stay until late Sunday night. Lester was almost always fishing. Mel occupied himself with getting out and exploring the countryside. Sometimes he loaded the big ATV in the bed of his truck and headed into the backwoods. Sometimes he threw the road bicycle in the truck and headed out to God knows where to ride some particularly challenging road he read about on the internet. Other times he took the motorcycle out on day rides. It was beautiful riding country, if quite often windy, but the wind came as part of the deal. It was a fact of life people in this area learned to accept and adapt to. Just as Mel had adapted to the Wyoming wind, so too was he adapting to life beyond L.A. and he began to feel at home.

I Ran to Alva

An Uneasy Truce

"You're sure that list is complete, Lester?" Terri asked.

"Yeah. Me and Mel went over it three times." He replied, holding it up for her to see. "This should be the whole job right here."

"OK, but remember the budget. Not a dime over two thousand, understand? Not a dime."

"Yeah Miss Terri, I know."

"Where's Mel?"

"Hookin' up to the trailer over yonder."

"OK, well, how long do you suppose you guys will be gone?"

"Can't rightly say. Depends on if they have anybody to help us load it up. If they do, we should only be an hour or two. If not, I reckon we'll be gone most of the day."

"Allright, well, just do your best."

They heard Mel's big Ford diesel rumble to life and he brought it around to pick up Lester. "Good to go?" he called to Lester through the open window. He could see Terri giving Lester some earnest instructions and felt a little sorry for him. Sometimes she just didn't know when to turn it off and he thought Lester was entirely too nice. Just once he'd like to see Lester turn and walk away from her in mid-sentence, but Mel figured that would never happen. Lester was just too much of a… gentleman. On second thought, that wasn't really such a bad thing. Considering all the snakes and other low-life's Mel had been surrounded by for so long, being around a gentleman was a refreshing change. He was a reminder that there were still good people in the world. For all Lester's simple ways and simple speech, how many people could use a lesson from him in good behavior? Most, he figured. Maybe he himself could use such a lesson. He decided to stop being so critical of Lester and just observe and… learn.

Lester ambled over to the truck and climbed in. "Let's burn rubber, there, hot rod!" he said with a laugh. They departed with a wave to Terri and headed out to Turner's Lumber Mill for the materials they needed. Lester casually gave Mel some directions to get them headed the right way and Mel figured the elder man would update him as they drove. The second turn of the journey put them on a road Mel hadn't yet driven, so he was soaking in the scenery as they went.

"This one fine truck, here, young man. Yes sir. I ain't never rode in a truck with such nice seats. I could live in this thing. I see how you'd like driving it cross country, no doubt."

"Thanks, it's been good so far. Pulls like a freight train, too. How much weight you figure we'll have on that trailer once it's loaded?"

"Mmmm, four ton, I reckon."

"You won't even feel the difference in this thing with that loaded trailer. Diesel power baby!" Mel said, laughing and patting the dashboard.

"I dunno," Lester countered. "Sure, it has pullin power, but it's a nasty ol' stinky thing, a diesel engine. All that clatterin', smokin', rattlin', sound like someone done dropped a bucket of bolts down in the oil pan and the engine is chewin' 'em all up," he finished with a chuckle.

Mel knew Lester was just giving him the business for a laugh and didn't mind playing along. He asked Lester a barrage of questions as they drove, about all the landmarks they passed and anything that caught his attention. Lester delighted in the younger man's curiosity and indulged his questions throughout the entire drive. As they drove on, Mel thought he felt an occasional vibration coming from the front end that he hadn't noticed before. As the miles passed, the vibration became more consistent and Mel noticed it was most noticeable under acceleration. Soon, Lester noticed it also.

"You ever heard that noise before?" he asked.

"Nope, just started about 10 miles ago. Crap."

"We'll check it out when we get to the mill; it's just a couple more miles. Maybe somethin' just come loose."

"Let's hope so."

Mel swung the truck and trailer into the lumber mill's large, open parking area and pulled off to the far side so as not to obstruct the huge commercial haulers coming and going.

"Lester, why don't you go in and talk to them about our order while I check out the truck? I don't think we should just go loading up the trailer until we know we can get it all back home."

"Yeah, all right then." Lester walked into the office and greeted everyone warmly. They'd all known each other for decades, especially Sally Turner, co-owner of the mill, whom Lester had known since Kindergarten as Sally Dresbach. She dropped what she was doing, called Lester to sit at her desk and went over his list meticulously. She asked him detailed questions about what they were trying to do with the materials, so as to give him the best bang for the buck. When it was all done, they were looking at a little over $2200 with tax and Lester looked at the floor.

"What's the matter, Les?" Sally asked him.

"Well, Miss Terri only give me a 2000 dollar budget – tops. I'm gonna have to cut some corners. Maybe substitute some spruce where we had the redwood on the list. Can we do that?"

"Miss Terri? Oh, you mean Terri Green who bought the Weaverly place?"

"Yeah, I stayed on there. I worked for Weaverly his last year there and he recommended she keep me, so she did."

"Is she from the city or something, Les?"

"I reckon so. She from Oregon, but yeah, I don't see her as a country girl by upbringin'. She catchin' on fast, though. Why you ask?"

"Well, sticking hard and fast to a number like she told you. We know life out here ain't like that, don't we?"

"Oh sure, but I don't think she just negotiatin'…I think it's really all the money she got for this project here. She pretty good at pinchin' pennies, so I think she just lookin' at the money."

"Well….allright then my friend, tell you what. I got a shipment in last week from a Washington lumber mill that went out of business and I can sell it to my friends for less because I don't have any milling time in it. A 15% discount will get you under your budget and get you the really good wood you need to do this thing right."

"Oh Sally, you is a good one. Yes you are."

"You're the good one, Les, my friend. You always were a good one,"she smiled broadly and patted his hand. "Now let me get this order entered in so we can get you all loaded up."

"Oh! I need to check with Mel on the truck," he remembered.

"Mel?"

"He's the new boy Miss Terri hired this spring. We drove his truck up here with the trailer, but it started makin' some funny noises just a few miles back. He's out there now lookin' at it to see if it's anything serious.'

"Oh, well let me call back and get my nephew Dylan to go out there and look at it. He's a wizard with trucks and stuff, maybe he can help."

"Dylan… I don't know."

"Lester, give him a chance. He isn't always a hot head. He's been a great help to us here at the mill."

"I know Sally, but… well, the story is he and Mel had a run in before at Ruby's over in Hulett."

She thought about that. She had heard a whisper of a story about Dylan belittling a new guy in town, but not more detail than that. This guy Mel accompanying Lester must have been the guy. "I'll just go out with him to set expectations. Maybe you can walk out before me and put a few words into your man Mel."

"Allright Sally, maybe you got a good plan there." But Lester was not at all certain of his words. Dylan Turner had already accumulated a decade's worth of reputation as a bully and a hot head. He had to be the big dog in the room and made damn sure everyone knew it. And he wasn't sure that would sit with Mel. The story was that Dylan backed him down that day in Ruby's, but working with Mel, Lester hadn't seen anything in the young man to suggest he would back down. There was just such a quiet, solid confidence about the man. That day Dylan came to pick up some barley hay while he and Miss Terri were gone, while Mel was fixing that rusted water pipe, Dylan had broken the step ladder and then just… voluntarily… run off to the store and bought a new one. Something he was not known for doing. And Lester began to consider bigger picture. He wondered, for real, if Mel and Dylan had had a run in that day. Maybe something left over from the run-in at Ruby's? Hmmm…

So he headed out to check on Mel and see if he had made any discoveries and repairs to the truck. He found Mel standing next to it, talking on his cell phone, clearly frustrated. From what Lester could glean, Mel was conversing with a repair shop about something to do with the truck's front driveshaft that provided power to the front axle for the four wheel drive. Finally, Mel simply said "Thanks" into the phone and ended the call.

"No luck?" Lester asked.

"Well, I think I figured out what's wrong. I think it's one of the u joints between the transfer case and the front axle. On older trucks, I could just disconnect that drive shaft and roll along with two wheel drive until I could fix it, but not this truck. It doesn't work like that."

Lester considered making a humorous remark about the big, rugged diesel that Mel had bragged on only a few minutes before, but figured now was probably not the time.

"Hello Mel, I am Sally Turner," she greeted him warmly. "I have been a friend of Lester's here since we were just school kids. I understand you have a problem with your truck?"

"Yes ma'am," he greeted her warmly. "I think I know what's wrong with it, but it's a long story.'

"Well, I asked my nephew Dylan – Lester said you two already met – to come out here and take a look. He's been building and repairing custom trucks since he was a kid, so maybe he can help. If you two can get along for a bit," she added with the authority of a wise older woman addressing a younger boy.

"Ahh, yes ma'am, well, I don't see why we can't get along," he replied, as he spied Dylan walking across the driveway.

"Mel," was all Dylan said with a nod of his head when he greeted him.

"Dylan," was Mel's terse response.

"Whatcha got goin' on?"

"I think one of the front u joints is shot, but a shop told me I can't just remove it like the old days and drive in two wheel drive."

"That's true. The Powertrain Control Module will freak out and will keep trying to apply four wheel drive until it burns out the actuator."

Mel sighed at the futility of it, but clearly Dylan understood the problem.

"But I know what I can do," Dylan thought aloud. "I'll disconnect the plug to the driveshaft sensor and wire it directly to ground. That will defeat any signal it tries to send to the PCM. So we could disconnect the front driveshaft until you get some new u joints in there. Mind if I have a look?" Dylan said, gesturing to the truck.

"Please," Mel said cordially.

For a big guy, Dylan slid deftly under the Ford and the three others could hear the metallic clunking of the loose drive shaft as the big man tugged and pulled at it. "Yeah, definitely the u joints, you were right. " He slid out from under the truck. "You got any tools to remove it?"

"Sure do, I got a box in the bed."

"Why don't you start in on it and I'll go to our shop and get a length of wire and some connectors so I can ground that switch."

"Sounds like a plan." So Mel walked to the bed of the truck to retrieve the necessary tools as Dylan walked back toward the mill's shop.

Lester and Sally stood looking at each other, perplexed at the young mens' cordial behavior with each other while considering the stories they'd heard. Lester just shrugged his shoulders at Sally and smiled. Mel dove under the truck with a handful of tools and began wrenching on the driveshaft. Removing it was not a very complicated procedure and he had it out just in time for Dylan's return. Dylan looked at the shaft, evaluated the u joints and merely nodded affirmation. Then he went under the truck with the length of pre-fabricated wire and connectors he'd made in the shop. In a couple minutes he was done and emerged from under the big Ford with a satisfied look.

"So when you get the new u joints installed," he addressed Mel, "just remove the wire I connected and then you need to plug that white connector back into the side of the transfer case. You'll see it hanging there when you go back under to do the work. Real simple."

"Cool. I appreciate it Dylan, really." And Mel extended his hand to shake.

"Yeah, well, it's no problem at all." And he received Mel's outstretched hand and briefly made eye contact as they shook. The moment was an unspoken communication between the two men. Each was of the opinion that they were the top dogs in their respective worlds, but they didn't necessarily have to be combatants. "So your order is being filled now. Just pull up next to the building and the guys will load your trailer."

"Oh, you're gonna load it?" Mel seemed surprised.

"You think I'd make this old man load all that wood?" Sally laughingly observed with a wink to Lester. "You go park that thing and then come on in to the office for some iced tea while my boys get it loaded and strapped down nice and proper."

"Fantastic idea," he said, smiling to Sally.

"See ya around Mel," Dylan said cordially as he turned to walk back toward the mill.

"All right Dylan thanks again for the help." He got into the truck and rolled it slowly over to the loading area.

As Lester and Sally walked together to the office, they mused at how the young men seemed to get along so well, but Lester's mind was working. Something didn't add up here. He'd known Dylan since he was a snot nosed kid throwing rocks at birds in the church parking lot. He was never just nice to anyone, no matter the circumstances, not even his favorite aunt standing there with the expectation that he was going to behave. Even that was not enough to control a man of Dylan's ego and physical stature. No. Something happened between him and Mel, something besides the confrontation in Ruby's diner. Had to have been that day Dylan broke the ladder at Miss Terri's place. Dylan didn't have a generous bone in his body. Something happened that day. The question for Lester was should he press Mel about it?

I Ran to Alva

Of Fairs and Successes

July had been a month of successes, large and small. On the small end of things, Lester had wandered into a farm equipment auction house down south of Sundance just because he liked to look at stuff. Men like to tease women about how much time they spend shopping, but the truth is men will do the very same thing when presented with goods they like. So it was with Lester. He wandered through the place for at least a half hour with not the least intent to buy anything. In the loading dock, he saw two men working to unload a large flatbed truck under the direction of a store employee. He casually walked over to peek at what they had to offer. They had unloaded three large implements with the shop's forklift. Lester knew what two of them were but not the third. He kept staring at it; certain he could figure it out. He was about to ask one of the men about it when he saw a post hole digger still in the flatbed. It had a frame around it, indicating that it was meant to be operated with a conventional tractor's three point hitch and power take off (PTO). The auger appeared to be an 8-inch bit, perfect for the size of posts he and Mel had talked about placing along the creek edge.

"You fellas not droppin' that off?" Lester asked, pointing to the auger.

"Naaa," the younger of the two answered. "Gonna drop it off at the scrap yard on the way home. The 3-point frame is busted in two spots and daddy says he just doesn't feel like welding it. Besides we done sold the tractor, so got no use for it. We'll just take what the scrap yard will pay for the metal."

"How much you reckon they'll give ya for it?"

"Daddy said about 35 bucks."

Lester's mind was working. He'd heard Mel brag on and on about his welding skills and he knew Mel had a welder, though he hadn't had an opportunity or need to use it yet. "Other than them two spots to be welded, does it still work?"

"Oh heck yeah." The young man partly lifted it and spun the input shaft by hand. The universal joint and the gear box turned freely and without noise or any wobbling. "You interested?"

Lester scratched his chin, deliberately pausing.

"You know what? You'll save me a 15 minute trip out of my way. It's yours for 20 bucks."

It was all he could do to keep from smiling. "Well, I reckon that's fair. I'm sure I can find someone to weld it up for me. It might come in handy for some work I need to do." He slowly, calmly pulled the twenty dollar bill out of his wallet and handed it to the younger man as if he was still uncertain. "Can I talk you two young studs inta loadin' it in my pickup? My back ain't so good," he lied.

"Not a problem pops," the younger man smiled. They drove the flatbed out, set the auger in Lester's old Dodge and drove away happy - but not as happy as Lester.

Mel's July windfall came when he took the ATV out for some off road exploring and had gotten lost. He knew generally where he was, but it was pretty obvious that the road he was on was not where he expected it. This became evident when he happened on a small, ancient looking sawmilling operation with a house and barn next to it. An elderly man and woman outside stopped whatever they'd been doing to watch him approach. He decided to ask them where he was and hopefully make a pleasant introduction. He rolled up to them slowly, shut the engine off and removed his helmet. He smiled broadly as he climbed out of the ATV and said, "I'm a little lost. Would you mind telling me what road I'm on? It doesn't show up on my GPS," he concluded holding up his iphone with the map displayed.

"Well, that's cuz it ain't no road," the elderly woman replied somewhat cheerfully. "It's our driveway."

Mel was stunned. "But I turned out of that dry creek bed 4 miles back and came here."

The old man laughed. "Yep. If you'd a turned right instead of left, you'd a gone about a mile and hit the road you was lookin' for."

"Wow," Mel said, he was beginning to grasp the enormity of their property, "this is amazing. Well, I am sorry for trespassing. I didn't mean to."

"Don't you worry about it now sweety," she replied. "Actually, we don't get too many visitors back up in here, so it's nice to see a friendly face. You from around here?"

"Oklahoma originally, but I'm working on a small ranch over in Alva."

"You don't say?" the old man smiled. "I growed up over around there, and Hulett. So did Margie," he said, pointing to the woman.

"Margie?" Mel replied, "Pleased to meet you, I'm Mel. Your name sir?"

"Oh, yeah, I'm Stanley," and they both shook Mel's hand. "We been up here since we was younger'n you. It was my grandpappy's place. He left it to my daddy, but daddy wasn't much interested in it, so he just give it to us when we got married."

"Well, it's beautiful; I can see why you'd want to live here."

"Yep, but I'm gittin' too old to work the sawmill anymore, so we's figurin' to sell off the equipment and just sit on the porch all day," he winked at Margie.

"That sounds like a plan," Mel said, "I got a long time to go before I can look forward to that, myself."

"Yeah, well, just enjoy each year as it comes. Don't get in no rush for any particular thing. You rush things, you can mess 'em up you know." He affirmed.

"Like folding laundry," Margie chimed in. "Do it in a rush and you just wrinkle everything up, might as well not even have spent the time. Make each fold the right way."

Mel smiled the smile of a young man being politely and patiently schooled. These people had seen at least 70 years of life and knew what they were talking about. He soaked in the lesson and appreciated the intent.

"Don't s'pose you're in the market for any lumber millin' equipment?"

"Naawww," Mel said slowly. "We do need some tractor implements, if you got any."

"Nuthin' comes to mind." Stanley said, looking at the ground. "Got some good lumber, though, if maybe you need anything like that."

"Lumber…" Mel said, thinking about the small bridge he and Lester had recommended to Terri they should build. It was needed to span over the creek so the cows could safely go back and forth in times of high water. "You know, I do need some stuff for a bridge project, can I see what you got?"

Stanley and Margie walked him around the back of the mill and it took his breath away. Huge piles of logs, rails, beams, studs and posts, meticulously grouped by diameter and length.

"What kind of bridge you reckon to build?" Stanley asked.

Mel gave him a fairly detailed verbal description of what he and Lester had discussed. Margie could see what was coming next, so she retrieved a note pad and pencil. In barely two minutes, Stanley rendered a rather detailed drawing of the bridge Mel had pictured in his head. In another five minutes, he generated a list of materials, right down to the pier anchors. Mel was truly impressed at this seemingly simple country gent who had the mind of a civil engineer and the hands of a roughneck. It had been fun watching Stanley at work, but now they were going to get to talking price and he was going to be ashamed for wasting his time.

"Well, since I just wanna close it all down and if you do all the loadin' and haulin'…" he hesitated and looked at Margie," I reckon it might be on around 1200 bucks." Margie's eyes approved and Stanley nodded affirmation that his offer was good.

Mel was speechless; he had been expecting the price to be at least five thousand dollars. The mill over in Sundance had told him his project was likely to be around seven thousand, at full retail. He was certain that Terri would go for the 1200; she had mentioned that she might be able to squeeze three thousand in another couple months, so he figured there must be some amount, some portion of it, available now. And even if there wasn't, he could commit to it and she could slowly pay him back. This opportunity had to be seized, even though he knew he'd spend another 200 dollars in fuel for what would probably require three trips to get it all transported to Alva. "That's an amazing offer, Stanley. If you're sure, then I will accept."

His response told both Stanley and Margie that the young man knew what a screaming deal he had just made, and that he was grateful. They smiled at each other and then both shook Mel's hand again to affirm it. They exchanged contact information and made tentative plans for Mel's return to take the loads. Before he got ready to leave, he asked Stanley if he could take the drawing he'd rendered so he could show Lester and Terri. He agreed, but then Margie thought it ought not to be stuffed into his pocket, so she retrieved a large manila envelope and placed it inside without folding it. "No wrinkles," she said again to Mel. He thought the follow up lesson was charming and repeated, "No wrinkles."

Stanley gave him directions to get back to the road he was originally looking for and then he hopped into the big ATV and headed out. "Score," he said inside his helmet as he left, but really, he had enjoyed his time with Stanley and Margie just as much as stumbling into a great lumber deal.

The big score of July really belonged to Terri. She was antsy to tell Lester and Mel the news over their morning coffee on that last Friday morning. It had rained all night but stopped just minutes before, leaving everything soggy and cold, so they all went inside Mel's trailer. The two men never got a chance to speak.

"I have to tell you…" Terri began, deliberately pausing to build the drama. She seemed to like drama, Mel thought. "That huge farmer's market in Spearfish has chosen us as an egg contractor!" she practically screamed.

She threw open a smile wider than Mel had yet seen and…wow…was she pretty. Her eyes sparkled with enthusiasm and… warmth? That was interesting. He sat speechless, trying to process the significance of what she said and what it would mean. He was not familiar with being an egg contractor. Do you own the chickens? Lease them? Can you even lease chickens, he mused? But he got to staring at her eyes again and lost his train of thought.

Upon the announcement, Lester immediately turned to look at Mel to see if he understood or had any questions, but he was so amused at the younger man's deer-in-the-headlights expression that he just kept staring and didn't say anything at all.

"What? – Don't you guys know what this means?" she persisted with audible annoyance.

Mel jolted out of his stupor. "Well, it must be good, but honestly, no, I don't know the first thing about it."

"Hmm," she replied, feigning condescension, "and you call yourself an Oklahoma farm boy."

"I never said…"

"Whatever," she playfully cut him off. "I will explain it to you two heathens. They send out a crew to construct a first rate, stand-alone chicken barn. They provide the chickens. They even give an allowance for feed. We tend to the chickens, gather the eggs, box them and prepare them for their trucks to pick up. And they pay us money. They will send an inspector once a month, but as long as we are passing inspections, that's it."

"Actually, Miss Terri," Lester chimed in, "I am familiar with these arrangements."

"And?"

"You done real good. These are really hard to come by. The outfits who have 'em don't give 'em up easy. You ain't gonna get rich, but you can make decent money and it's steady money, month in and month out. Yes ma'am, that's a fine thing you done there." And he held his coffee cup up to propose a toast. "To Miss Terri, the Lady Duck who came to Alva and made a go of it."

They all smiled and clinked their coffee cups. Mel was completely oblivious to Lester's "duck" reference, but Terri was not. Somehow Lester had found out that she had attended Oregon University, home of the Ducks. That alone did not worry her, but she wondered what else he had learned, and how. She would need to know if any other information he knew could come back to haunt her. She did not suspect him to be the kind of man that would use information against people, but he might accidentally say something to someone, just as he had carelessly done with the toast. A sit-down with Lester was imperative.

"Well, that's great news!" Mel affirmed. "Nice job, boss. Maybe we won't have to file unemployment claims this winter." he said with a smile to Lester.

"Ohhh no, I have plans for you gentlemen all year. You won't have any more time to sit on your duffs in January than you do now."

The two men let out a collective groan which only made her laugh. She hadn't laughed much in the time Mel had known her and it was a shame. She had a high pitched laugh, very feminine and pleasing to a man's ear. Something a man would enjoy, but they quickly turned to the discussion of the day's work ahead and planned it all out, as always. When they finished, Terri had another announcement.

"The Crook County Fair is this week and I think we should all go. My little troop of 4-H girls has entered multiple things in the arts competitions and also has a couple entries in foods. I'd like for us all to go together and just hang out instead of being so focused on work all the time."

"That's a fine idea," Lester replied. "I reckon I ain't been to that fair in 15 years."

"Sounds great," Mel agreed. "When should we go?"

"Let's leave about six, we can stop and get a bite to eat on the way, my treat."

"That's nice of you." Mel allowed.

"Yeah, but you're driving," she countered. And Lester just laughed at how she so often played him. "Your truck is the fanciest thing rolling down this driveway, so we wanna go in style, right Lester?"

"Amen, Miss Terri, you speak the truth."

Mel saw he was outnumbered, but was actually happy to drive. The trio set about their respective tasks which meant that Terri would go back into her house for a few hours, working the phones and the internet and then driving off to meet people face to face. Mel and Lester handled their end of things with the usual teamwork and were pretty much done by four o'clock. Lester hopped in his old Dodge and drove home for a shower and change of clothes. His house was en route to the fair, so they would just pick him up along the way. Mel showered and chose his shirt deliberately - the short-sleeved one that still covered his tattoo, but also revealed the size and definition of his arms and shoulders. His sister had bought it and when she saw him wear it for the first time, told him that any woman who wasn't turned on, simply wasn't into men. He was wondering if that was true and was willing to take a shot at finding out. Once he was ready, he made a glass of iced tea and sat out at the dinette, waiting for Terri to walk out or text to let him know she was ready. He occupied his time looking at a large National Forest Service map that he'd spread open on the little table and planned his next outing on the ATV. Then he heard her footsteps.

When he looked up at her, the sun was hitting her from the front of her right side. Her eyes, which had already held his attention on more than one occasion, just popped in the sunlight, with no hat to shadow or diminish their reflection. Her hair color was no surprise, as he'd certainly seen it every day, but seeing it cast across her shoulders instead of pulled back into that tight ponytail was a bigger difference than he expected. She was, actually, a woman, and a beautiful one at that. Mel could only stare.

"What?" she interrupted his trance, pretending to be annoyed or oblivious to his mental state, but she knew what she had done. She was still of the mind that as long as Mel worked for her, nothing could ever happen between them, but it was nice to see that she could still elicit a reaction like that from a man her own age. Maybe someday, then, she'd still be able to turn the mens' heads when she was ready.

Mel knew that he'd telegraphed his sentiments and was resigned that there was no way to walk it back now. The genie was out of the bottle. OK, he thought, so be it. Well, let's see if little sister was right about his shirt. So he stood up, but bent at the waist so he could fold up the map on the table. As he did so, he made sure to move his arms in such a way that their definition would be obvious. Just before he was done, he looked up quickly and said "No wonder they've gone to GPS" with a big smile. The quick look up was rewarded; he had caught her eyes looking at him, actually evaluating him. She turned away quickly, but he had seen what he needed to see. And he muttered to himself "Thanks sis."

They walked to the truck side by side and he instinctively reached to open the door for her. She reacted with a playfully defiant look and a "Really?" He got the message, so he moved back, but carefully observed her form as she stepped up into the cab. The jeans she was wearing were just a tad more stylish and form fitting than any others he'd seen her wear, as was her blouse. The gal definitely had a figure. The shapely silhouette he saw that one night as she was backlit by the porch light was not an apparition and it looked even better in broad daylight. He took his place behind the wheel, fired up the big diesel and headed over to Lester's place. He was sitting on the front porch of his little house, dressed and ready to go. He looked quite dapper, all shaved, combed and dressed in upscale cowboy apparel. He climbed in the rear cab of the truck, made some funny comments about how handsome they all looked, but true to his form announced that he was in fact very hungry. They had a good dinner at the local BBQ joint and rolled over to the fair. The sun was still maybe a half hour from setting, but its heat was waning and the temperature was comfortable.

The fair was awash in customary noises of the games, the rides and the PA announcements going on over at the rodeo arena. Their first order of business was to go to the arts display inside the main exhibition hall and see the wares presented by Terri's 4-H girls. They walked slowly through the hall, admiring and commenting on many of the art entries. Occasionally, Terri recognized a name on an entry and would tell Mel and Lester a quick anecdote of that girl and the thing she had made. Mel noticed how with each girl, she told a personal detail that made them unique and why she had no trouble separating them from each other, though she'd only been involved with the group a few months. She really notices things in people, he thought.

One exhibit really caught Mel's eye. It was at the front of the table and the creator had cleverly placed a small battery powered LED behind it. It appeared to be multi-colored glass, almost two inches thick, but the light shining through it revealed the colorful form of a horse. He knelt down to have a really close look and Terri asked him why he thought it was so interesting. As he explained the view of the horse within, he was also baffled how the whole thing was made. He knew nothing about creating such things, so it was marvelous to him. She bent over a little to examine it also and offered a brief explanation of melting glass, forming it, etc. As she was talking, Mel became aware of her hair touching his shoulder and, briefly, the side of his face. It was a very delicate but powerful sensation and she smelled great, too. Far too soon, she finished her explanation and stood up. He continued to stay focused on the piece for another 5 seconds; long enough to let her casually walk away to look at the rest of the exhibits, but it had been a really good moment. An unexpected moment. Questions moved in his head.

The trio took their time enjoying all the home made crafts and art work. Lester and Mel were especially enamored by three metal pieces and stunned when they saw the owner ID tag that said he was only 14 years old. When Mel saw that, he went back over the welds with a discerning eye and was still impressed.

"Why you inspecting that kid's welds so close?" Lester asked.

"Because I'm jealous." Mel admitted. "Took me 10 years of practice to weld a bead like that and some days, I still can't."

Eventually, they saw all the exhibits, so they headed out to the midway to play some games and indulge the rides. No rides for Lester, he made that perfectly clear. His adamant statement that he would not ride anything caught Mel and Terri by surprise for its sincerity. They could only look at each other, smirk and shrug.

Mel blew through 20 bucks playing various games, secretly hoping to win some little trinket he thought Terri might like, to no avail. He knew he had to try again when they happened upon the baseball throwing game, because front and center was the grand prize – a three foot tall stuffed replica of a Palomino. Terri stood transfixed at the oversized "horse" and Mel saw the girlish want in her eyes. Winning it was next to impossible. Three baseballs cost five bucks. There were three stacks of three milk bottles each, arranged with two on the bottom and one on top. The object was to knock the three stacks down with one ball each. Even if a thrower had a dead-eye aim, the game was still rigged against him, as the bottles were filled with sand to make them heavy and resistant to movement. Mel knew all this. What the vendor didn't know was Mel had been a standout baseball pitcher in high school and junior college. Terri didn't know that either, but she was about to learn.

Mel asked the cocky young "carny" attendant if it was OK to back up a few feet to throw. He merely shrugged approval. Mel's first ball hit the left stack dead center and sent the sand-laden bottles flying. It startled the carny, as he had never seen that before. Terri was startled the moment the ball left Mel's hand as she heard it literally whiz through the air and crash into the stack. Before she could even draw a breath, he wound up and threw the second one with similar results. The carny thought to heckle Mel and break his focus as his boss had taught him to do, but before he could even get the words out, the third ball smashed into the remaining set of milk bottles and sent them careening in all directions. The deal was done, the horse was won. The once-cocky carny grudgingly climbed up the ladder, unwound the wires on the stuffed Palomino and handed it down to Mel. Terri was beyond excited and was bouncing in little rabbit jumps as she just "knew" he was going to hand it over to her. Only he didn't. Without thinking, she hugged and thanked him profusely. He got an amused look as he observed her outstretched arms and the look on her face that said she was expecting to receive it.

"What?" he asked, with a smile on his face.

"Well, can I have it?" she was practically pleading.

"But I won it. I want to put it next to the workout station in my trailer. I think he's very inspiring to look at and will motivate me when I'm working out," he teased. The crushed, pouty look on her face was more than he could stand, even for just those few seconds, so he handed it over.

She squealed like a school girl and threw her one free arm around his neck, jumping and squealing in his ear. In spite of the spectacle it was creating, he could have stood there for hours. She planted a kiss on his cheek and then released her hold. She held the stuffed Palomino at arms' length to admire it and then held it close again, smiling at Mel with those big twinkling eyes. His excitement in the light hearted moment was replaced by solemnity, looking at her in the multi-colored glow of the midway lights. All he wanted was to grab her and kiss her and hold her close, but even in the heat of this moment he was cool enough to know now was not the time. He even admitted to himself that there might not ever be a time, she might not ever be receptive to such an advance on his part, but then again she might, if he timed it right. And now was not the time.

Lester quietly observed all this from several feet away. He noted the look on Mel's face and wondered if he was seeing the blessing of a new relationship, or the preliminary stages of a train wreck. He hoped for the former, suspected the latter. Yet it was clear that tonight, these two needed space. Maybe they'd discover something with each other and maybe they'd talk about it and decide it was not to be. Either way Lester knew that tonight would be the culmination of things he'd seen building over the past couple months and he knew it could only come to fruition in his absence.

"Hey you two," he called out, "I'm goin' over to the livestock barn and see my old buddy from Belle Fourche. I'll catch up with you kids later." He turned and walked before they could question, argue, or offer to tag along.

"Let's go check out some rides," Mel implored.

"Cool."

They had a good time on the tiny roller coaster and the twirling, chain mounted swings, but it was the Tilt-O-Whirl where things got unexpectedly kicked into the next gear. They took their seats in the concave "cars" with Mel seated on Terri's right. The seating seemed irrelevant at the start, but as the machine got up to full speed, their positions became the catalyst for everything that happened over the next few minutes. The little cars whipped and twirled the occupants inside as the cars themselves got propelled around a guided path on the huge machine. Normally the occupants stabilize themselves inside by holding on to a bar in front of them, but Terri was holding the Palomino with one arm, leaving only the other arm with which to hold the bar. When the Tilt-O-Whirl hit full speed, she could not hold herself in place. The g-forces pushed her into Mel and she did not have the strength to pull herself away. She felt a moment of fear as she started to slide and wondered if she would have to release the prize Palomino to save herself. Wedged against his shoulder and upper arm, she could feel the tautness of his body and how it did not move or jiggle in spite of the car's near-violent motion. He felt like an anchor holding her in place. It was obvious that as long as she was wedged against him, he was going to hold them both in place and she needn't worry about the pony, or herself.

The Tilt-O-Whirl continued to toss them about, but she became oblivious to its forces. Without thinking or even wondering why, she turned to look up at Mel who was already waiting to make eye contact. She was drawn to him and moved her face up to kiss him. When their lips made contact, they were no longer aware of the machine's spinning gyrations, but became enveloped in the hurricane of their long, wet kiss. The wild ride had come to a near standstill before either of them noticed that it had slowed at all. They separated and prepared to disembark. When it came to a complete stop and the operator announced the way and means by which they should depart, Mel was all smiles and reached for Terri's hand to assist her out of the little car. She would not take it, did not make eye contact and walked past him without saying anything. He knew, instantly, that she regretted it. And he had a flashback to that night with the tractor, how she had come home so grumpy and had been so cold to him and Lester, yet only a couple hours later was sweetness and light. This up and down, this roller coaster as it were, was nothing new to him and was something he should have seen coming. Literally two minutes ago, they were locked into a passionate kiss that he believed was a long time in the making. If she regretted it now, surely the sentiments that spawned the regret must have already been known to her beforehand, so why kiss him at all? And she did, didn't she? She looked up at him and kissed him. Then stalked off, obviously regretting what she had done. What the hell was her deal?

He walked after her, keeping a few feet of space behind her so that she wouldn't feel smothered. They walked all the way to the opposite end of the midway where the lights and sounds began to diminish before she stopped, knowing he had followed her.

"Mel," she said without turning to look at him, "I am sorry for what happened there. And I am really really sorry if you feel I misled you." She turned slowly to face him. "I never meant for that to happen. Look, I am not in a place where I can get involved right now, especially with…"

"An employee?" he cut her off. He did feel betrayed a little, but he knew and could feel that her hesitance was deep and conflicted, she wasn't just being fickle. So he was able to give her a little bit of slack, but not much.

"I didn't mean it like that, I just…" and she stopped talking as tears rolled down her cheeks. He instinctively moved in to hug her, but she put her hand against his chest to keep him at a distance. He didn't try to push through the resistance, but he did believe it was time to give her something to think about.

"Terri…... what happened a couple moments ago was you and me acting on what we wanted without over thinking it, without any baggage. Those were your and my unfiltered wants and desires in action. Then when the ride was over, you let all that baggage, whatever it is, creep back into your mind. That's fine, I get it. We all carry something. You know from that kiss how I feel about you Terri and I know how you feel about me. I felt it and you can't hide it, but I'm not going to beg you for anything, 'cuz one thing my Grandpa taught me is a person is only going to give you what they are willing to let go. And right now, you're holding on to everything. So I will tell you this: You know how I feel about you from the way I kissed you. It's there and it will stay there until the moment I decide that you will not be able to let go of the baggage. If I make that determination, if the day comes when I decide that you are simply not going to be able to let go, then I will move on. But as long as I believe you're working on it, considering it, then what you felt when I kissed you will be there."

She did not look at him, but only nodded her head as he saw her tears dot the bare dirt at her feet. She allowed her arm to bend a little and he moved gently forward to hug her. They stood silent and motionless for a couple minutes as she composed herself, until she finally stood up straight and looked at him. "You're not wrong, Mel. Everything you said is true, especially the part about the baggage. I hope one day I can open it all up, let it all go, but I don't know Mel. I came out here in the middle of nowhere, away from everyone and everything I know, exactly so I would never meet anyone, never want anyone and never desire anyone. I can't promise you Mel that one day, for sure, I will be able to let it all go. I won't lie to you." And she managed a smile, "But you really have surprised me tonight. Right here, right now, I honestly didn't think you were…this sweet," she finished as she touchéd his cheek.

"Now I am insulted," he said with a smile. "How could you not know I was sweet after giving up the grand prize that I won with my own skill and derring-do? He was going to be the center piece of my exercise area and I gave him up to you just because you batted your eyes at me. How could you not know I was sweet?"

She stared at him a long moment. "Well, let's find Lester and see what he's up to."

"Yes of course," he said with a smile. And he didn't try to hold her hand as they walked back toward the midway.

I Ran to Alva

Full Speed Ahead

As August approached, Mel saw something on the 'Net about
the Sturgis motorcycle rally occurring soon. He was really
excited about that. He'd known about it since he was a kid,
always thought of going since the time he bought his first big
street bike and now here he was, living and working only a
couple hours away. He could go and not even stay the night if
he didn't want to. As he checked out more info, he decided to
indulge the full experience and camp overnight at "The Chip",
the Buffalo Chip Campground which is ground zero for so
many happenings in Sturgis. The week before the rally
commenced, Mel bought a large camp bag from an on-line
motorcycle store that was specifically built for his Triumph.
When it arrived, he spent an hour or so that evening after
dinner attaching it to the bike and then filling it with this and
that to see what was the most efficient way to pack it. Terri
watched from the office window for a while, curious what he
was up to. He hadn't said anything about going anywhere and
she was hopeful he wasn't going to ask for any extra time off.
The meat market in Belle Fourche had purchased 40 head of
cattle and she was going to need both of the men around next
week to deliver them, 8 at a time in the livestock trailer. It was
her largest sale yet and could really get her noticed by other
regional markets.

The next morning at their coffee, she made a point to ask Mel
about the motorcycle and the bag. He explained that he was
going to go overnight Saturday and would be back Sunday

evening. Terri was relieved on one hand but concerned on the other.

"Why do you want to go to that motorcycle rally? All those loud bikes and scary people…"

"Judge much?" he replied with a snicker.

"Touche,"she replied. "All I mean is it seems like it would just be chaos."

"Perhaps, but I've always wanted to see it. And I can handle the chaos, I think."

"I just don't see it."

Lester looked at the ground and snickered.

"Terri," Mel said with a calm solemnity, "You don't have to see it. And I wish you'd stop acting like I need your approval."

"You don't need my approval. I'm your employer, that's all, I know that. I just hear things about what goes on at that event."

Internally, Mel kinda cringed at her comment about her being his employer. He felt as though he had pushed too hard and subsequently pushed her into a corner. And she pushed back. He regretted making her do that.

"Terri," he began more patiently, "Yeah, I've heard the stories, but every large event has its fringe element. The rally grows every year. Would it keep growing if it was just the Wild Wild West? I don't think so. I'll be fine," he smiled.

She was not consoled. "Suit yourself."

"Allright you two," Lester interrupted, "let's get to work."

They performed all their customary tasks that day and for the remainder of the week. By Friday, Mel was all set with the stuff he was going to pack and take along with him on the motorcycle. Friday night after dinner, he made final preparations so he could take off Saturday as soon as everything was done. He was hoping to be on the road by 11 am. Lester hung around Friday after their work was done and Mel grilled up some burgers and corn on the cob, coated in butter and wrapped in foil to protect from the open flame. The two men enjoyed a leisurely meal, along with a couple stouts and good conversation.

"So let me see this bike you gon' ride over there. I ain't never really seen it since you started preppin' for this trip."

"Gladly," Mel replied. They walked over to where it was chained to the trailer and removed the cover. Mel explained the couple extra pieces of framework he'd welded to the rear of the bike to enable it to safely and securely carry a heavily-loaded bag. Lester thought the bike didn't look well suited to distance traveling, lacking as it was any kind of windshield or protective bodywork as he saw on most motorcycles designed for long, consecutive days on the road. Still, he figured Mel was a strong young man and could probably cope just fine for the relatively short hop over to Sturgis.

"I wish you well, young man. Just don't go joining any motorcycle gangs ok?" he said with a wink.

"No worries about that. I'm just going to brush up against that lifestyle, I guess, not immerse myself in it."

The next morning, Lester arrived as usual and the trio had their coffee meeting to talk over the few things they'd do, and also make tentative plans for Monday. Terri reminded them both that she'd be going to see her uncle again and might possibly be staying with him though Monday, if she was needed to assist him after having some serious medical tests run, but if the docs decided the tests were unnecessary, then she'd be home Sunday night, as usual. Lester affirmed he'd simply be out fishing at his favorite secret spot. She handed the men their paychecks and thanked them for another successful week.

"You could pay us electronically, you know. You could just set up automatic deposit and save yourself the time and nuisance of writing a physical check," Mel observed.

"No I can't," she countered. "Cro Magnon man over there doesn't have a real bank account and isn't interested in getting one."

Lester just shrugged.

"What?" Mel asked, laughing.

"Don't trust 'em," Lester said defiantly. "I ain't lettin' 'em holds my money, no sir."

Mel and Terri just looked at each and shrugged.

"So he takes his check to the bank and cashes it," she explained.

"Then what?" Mel asked. "What do you do with the cash? How do you secure it? What if someone steals it all? Do you starve until your next check?"

"It ain't as complicated as you think, young man. There's many ways to secure valuables. Maybe one day I'll tell ya 'bout it."

"Fair enough," Mel conceded.

"Besides," Terri allowed, "it would cost me another twenty bucks a month to set that up for you guys, so it's saving me a little money."

"Well, if cave man there ever decides to join the 21st century," Mel teased, "Please sign me up for direct deposit. Taking these things to the bank is a pain."

"Speaking of cave men," Terri said without missing a beat, "are you all ready for your trip over to Sturgis?"

"Here we go," he huffed, but knew she was just playing around.

"Seriously," she said "try to leave enough time to see Rushmore. It's even better than all the hype."

"Been there?" Mel asked.

"Yep, my first week here, I drove over there to look at it. Morning light is best, I think, but whatever, just go see it."

"Yeah, you should." Lester confirmed. Leave enough time to check out the unfinished Crazy Horse work, too."

At that, they all started in on their daily duties and Mel was finished by 9:30. He quickly dove into the shower, dressed in the riding clothes he'd already laid out, threw the last minute items on the bike and headed out.

"Careful!" Terri called to him, with a wag of her finger. He thought her admonition was a tad more serious than it needed to be, but he just blipped the Triumph's throttle and laughed at her. It was a great feeling to head up the road, all alone on just his bike, heading to an iconic event he'd dreamed of seeing since he was a boy. The weather was a tad hot, but felt perfect on a moving motorcycle. Just a couple miles up, he turned east onto Highway 24 and was surprised to see a smattering of motorcycles already heading the same direction. He waited for them to pass, there must have been 20 of them, and then pulled out behind them. They rolled along for maybe 10 miles until his turn onto County Road 86. The pack kept going. He knew from researching the route that they were probably going the more scenic path, but since it was his first time, he opted for simplicity. Just a half dozen miles down Road 86 was Interstate 90, where he'd get on the super slab and roll all the way to Sturgis. When he got to I-90, what he saw took his breath away.

All he could see, dotting the landscape for miles in either direction, were motorcycles. Not hundreds of them – thousands. He merged into a gap and rolled along with this particular pack at their speed. Everyone around him greeted him with a subtle nod of the head or slight wave of the hand. The group he was riding with was comprised mostly of Harleys it seemed. Some were stripped down Sportsters, some were the uber-luxurious Electra Glides, but most were something in between. The bikes in the pack and the bikes passing them by had license plates from every state in the West. He figured it made sense that would be the case since he was heading east to get there. The pack seemed content to stay in the right lane and move along at a sedate 65mph. This suited Mel for a while, but two things began to change his thoughts. One, the pack of Harleys he was in was exceptionally loud. He noticed that the helmetless and quarter-helmet wearers had ear plugs inserted. No doubt. Mel had no ear plugs and the noise was actually beginning to bother him. Two, there were other packs passing by at about 10-20 mph faster. His normal cruising speed was 75-80, partly because at that speed, the Triumph twin was spinning at an rpm range where it just felt a little smoother. Smoothness means less rider fatigue, so it had become his preferred riding speed on an open highway.

Soon he pulled out of the pack, moved to the left lane and gently accelerated away from them with a wave as he did. The bike seemed happy thrumming along at 75mph and he hoped it was just slow enough to not attract any attention from law enforcement. Before long another group came up behind, passed him and he decided to join in. He didn't stay with them long, however, as their ranks were comprised primarily of Ducatis and other sport bikes often referred to as crotch rockets. Their cruising speed was well into the mid-80-mph range, just a bit too high for Mel. So he throttled back and let them go. It became an accordion type of pattern where he would overtake slower groups, but there were always groups overtaking him, so he had to keep a diligent eye on his mirrors to move out of their way in time. When they were still 20 miles from Sturgis, the entire highway got congested with the sheer volume of motorcycles. Average speed slowed to 60mph, but Mel was happy that it was still moving. He remembered the LA traffic and how it was normal to encounter stop and go, for miles, at any time of the night or day. This 60 mph cruise was just fine by him.

Eventually, he started seeing signs for the Buffalo Chip campground and was stunned at the number of other riders that headed the same direction. Once at the entrance to The Chip, the entry line was so long and moving so slowly that he just shut off the Triumph's engine and paddled it forward with his legs a few feet at a time. He was thankful that he'd taken the time to buy and install the water bottle cage on the handlebar cross mount. The insulated water bottle was doing its job nicely, as each sip he needed was as cool as the one before.

"Hey," a woman called to him. She was on a Harley just a few feet behind and to his left. "Would you mind letting me have a sip?"

He turned to look and hand her the bottle. "No problem." Oh, and she was a looker. Low cut leather top, tan, lean arms and skin tight jeans. Just the sight of a woman like that on a motorcycle made him smile.

She took a drink and handed back the bottle, "Thanks man."

At any other time, he'd have used the opening as a means to strike up a dialog, to start "running his game" as he and his single buddies in LA used to say, but his head and his heart just weren't in it. The excitement of being at Strugis, with so much to see in such a short time, combined with the events of the last several months, made it almost impossible to even think about a relationship. Yeah, he thought of Terri occasionally and even allowed himself to admit that he was curious about her in that regard, but he wrote it off as simple curiosity because he was around her so often.

Eventually he got through the entrance line, was directed where to pitch his tent and got his "camp" all set up. His admission fee also got him a storage locker, where he placed anything he wasn't going to carry with him. Then he started strolling around The Chip. There was so much to see; the burnout contest, where riders would deliberately spin the rear tires until they started smoking and would just keep spinning them until they burned through all the rubber on the tire, and popped. He had smelled burnt rubber before, but not to this degree. It was so acrid that it involuntarily crinkled his nose and made it almost impossible to breathe normally. And he was 60 feet away from the burnout stage. The crowd surrounding the stage was absolutely thick with people. How could they stand it?

He moved on to the Chili cook off, the BBQ cook off and a dozen other cook offs that he would not have imagined. There was a stage for a bikini contest that was presently occupied by an upscale maker of leather jackets, chaps, vests and boots. Tiny little models paraded the wares back and forth to the hoots and hollers of all in attendance. Of course, every 50 feet there was another beer vendor and he spotted at least 8 stages where live bands performed everything from metal to country to rap. And any remaining available real estate was occupied by vendors of motorcycle parts and accessories. There were hundreds. Anything you wanted for a motorcycle, anything at all, could be bought here AND installed on the spot. As he looked around and took a mental step back, it occurred to him that this place was nothing but a flat level field. Two weeks ago it was probably bare grass, and then the preparations began. And now all the people were here. In 4 or 5 days, it would probably be a bare grass field again. The logistics of it all astonished him. It took him about 3 hours to walk one circuit around the "midway" as he thought of it, stopping to get a stout and what was advertised as a genuine german bratwurst. It was true to its billing and he noted that the vendor had travelled all the way from Wisconsin to be here. Upon completing his circuit of the midway, he decided to get on the Triumph and head into downtown Sturgis. He was prepared to be patient and to deal with a heavy, heavy crowd. Good thing he had prepared.

Upon leaving the Chip, he was only able to ride just fast enough on his way into town to maintain forward momentum so he didn't have to put his feet down. Bikes by the thousands and of every color, size and shape imaginable were crawling along the road in both directions. He reminded himself that this WAS why he came. He had expected massive crowds, and that meant moving slowly and being patient. He eventually got into the heart of town itself and was amused at the creative ways the police were allowing the motorcycles to park. It made sense, after all, how can riders dismount and patronize the local establishments if they can't park somewhere. It was a far cry from his memories of cruising Hollywood on a few Saturday nights. The cops on foot would walk along and enforce parking laws on motorcycles to the letter. If they could wedge a credit card between a motorcycle's rear tire and the curb, they wrote a parking ticket. Pricks all, but not here. People walking past the cops all greeted them, some patted them on the shoulder, and none spoke any word of disrespect. Very cool, Mel thought.

Suddenly a flashlight caught his attention, pointed at his eyes from a few feet away. A police officer shouted to him, "Space available!" Mel nodded and moved over to park the Triumph, thanking the officer. He set his helmet on the gas tank, not the least bit worried that someone would walk away with it. Such was the code at biker rallies. The sidewalks and streets were teeming with people in various states of inebriation, but even the cold sober folks were having a great time. It occurred to him that he was probably one of the cleanest cut men in town and yet he didn't feel the least bit out of place. Now and then a young lady would walk by, clad in just enough clothing to not be arrested, overtly flirtatious and Mel made sure to smile and deliberately raise his eyebrows in approval. Such was Sturgis etiquette.

As he approached one particular bar, the music blasting through the open doors and windows was reminiscent of the late Stevie Ray Vaughn. It was enough to make him stop walking and get in line to go inside. The wait was only 20 minutes and well worth it. Once inside he got a glass of stout and maneuvered as close to the stage as he could. The band was excellent, the people were rockin' and he was in the thick of the good times at Sturgis. A smile was pasted on his face as most of the young women who passed by would spin a few dance steps for his amusement and even their accompanying husbands or boyfriends didn't seem to mind. He felt the stress and the pain just melt away. Even though this was not truly his scene in a permanent way, he was somehow at home. He was… completely anonymous. He was not looking around to see who recognized him and what they might say to him if they did. There were thousands more interesting things and people to see, he was just part of the background. Happily so.

It wasn't long before he realized he had already put down four, or was it five, stouts and was feeling a little clumsy. And it occurred to him that at some point he had to ride back to his place at the Chip. So the next time the barely legal and barely dressed waitress came around, he ordered a Coke. After another couple hours of revelry and bottled water, he tipped the waitress a $50 bill which earned him a very visible lip print on the cheek, and he left. The main street was still roaring with action, though by now, some of the partiers had taken it too far. The polite but professional police had a couple paddy wagons parked on either end of town to aid in detaining those whom they had arrested and were going to process at the local gray bar hotel. He walked slowly, looking at all the custom bikes lined along the street and the people associated with them. Some were obviously hand built on a budget and were absolutely no frills, known as "throwbacks," their name paying homage to a time when motorcycles were customized by riders of limited budget and facilities. Others were specialized and customized to the point that Mel wondered why they even rode them on the street. Every single part on them was either chrome, stainless, polished copper or paint so flawless and deep that DaVinci himself would have said "Damn!" Mel could not imagine riding such a machine on a public street, as even the most routine of lay-downs would take weeks and tens of thousands of dollars to repair.

After a while of walking and sipping on a bottled lemonaid, he was pretty sure he was sober enough for the ride back. He laughed, though, when he spotted a portable breathalyzer machine that a guy was charging $2.00 per "blow" for you to find out if you were under the legal limit. As he stood there for a second, he learned that it printed a receipt with your own blood alcohol content (BAC) listed on it and a guarantee that if you failed a police administered test within 15 minutes of taking their test, they paid all your court costs plus $100,000.

So he ponied up the two bucks and blew into the machine. It said he was below the legal limit, which he suspected anyway, but wanted the receipt as a novelty to show Lester when he returned home tomorrow. Home? Is that what it had become? In such a short time? Interesting thought.

He meandered back in the general direction of where he remembered parking the Triumph and found it after a few minutes. Fortunately, the traffic headed out to the Chip was actually kind of light because most people were not ready to head back just yet. He enjoyed the short ride in the cool night air, but could have probably made the ride without the aid of his headlight, for all the auxiliary lighting units along the route. When he arrived, he retrieved all his gear from the rental locker and settled in to the tent, then checked email via his iphone and also saw that he had missed a call from his mom. As usual, she didn't leave a voice mail. He could only smile at her persistent reluctance to leave voice mails. In all the years he'd known her, she hated the way she clammed up and felt so awkward when speaking to a machine, so she just wouldn't do it. He made a mental note to call her in the morning. Unlike the vast majority of revelers, he hadn't come here to see how late he could stay up and how drunk he could get. He just wanted to get a feel for it and then get up early to take some of the best known and prettiest rides in the country. He could always come back next year and spend more time if the mood struck him. Next year? Would he be here next year? No sense worrying about it now, he thought. So he set the alarm on the iphone, crawled into the sleeping bag and called it a night.

The iphone's programmed dulcet tones awoke him promptly at 6am, but he pushed it out to another half hour. When that alarm also came, he was ready to get up and move. He made quick work of the tent and all the gear and was rolling by 7am - one of only a handful of people up that early in a sea of sleeping humanity. He rolled with a purpose toward Mount Rushmore, remembering Terri's recommendation to see it in the morning light. He stopped at a 24 hour diner for a quick breakfast and then stayed on the bike until he pulled into the parking lot beneath the four gargantuan heads carved into the South Dakota mountains.

Terri was right. The morning sun was at such an angle as to cast shadows on the faces, giving them almost life-like quality. And their backdrop was an impossibly blue, cloudless sky. He took at least 50 pictures from every angle he could think of, even asking another rider to take his pic aboard the Triumph with the heads in the distant background. He also took the time to read the various placards describing how Gutson Borglum designed it all and then led the team of heroic men who blasted the amazing shapes out of the raw rock. He wondered how many environmental impact reports would have to be filed with the Environmental Protection Agency if a person wanted to undertake such an effort these days. He reasoned as how it could probably never be done. Ever. He also read the placards about each of the presidents represented and learned a few things about each. He'd never been much of a history buff, but being in a place like this made the history so real, so right in your face, that it was fascinating. He got a cup of coffee from the visitor center and sat out on a bench, taking it all in as he sipped the hot brew. When he was done, he decided to get some kind of a memento form the gift shop and decided on a shot glass. A small item like that would be easy to pack home and could be easily displayed in the limited space in his trailer.

And if someone wanted to use it to throw back a little Jose Cuervo, all the better.

He finally had to tell himself it was time to leave, given the circuitous scenic route he'd planned for the return trip. And besides, it was starting to get kinda crowded. So he rolled the Triumph South and settled in for a couple hundred miles of scenic, twisting roads. The badlands and the mountains did not disappoint. These were prime motorcycle roads, though a bit crowded with the summer tourists and his fellow Sturgis fans. He made a decision to come back here when the tourist season was over. Maybe even take the exact same route. He saw where Custer fatefully made his last stand and had a lunch break at Wind Cave national Park, though he declined to take the tour, owing to the timeline to get home. The roads were magnificent, each more scenic and curvy than the last. He wondered if it was possible that he might wear out the shoulders of the Triumph's tires before the center. What a blast! For those hours, there was no LA, there was no history, there was nothing. It occurred to him that maybe he had actually tapped into the spirit of what he'd heard others speak about when riding motorcycles. That everything just disappears. He'd never been a "biker." A motorcycle was just something fun and different to ride, added a little spice to the travels compared to the comforts of a sedan or an SUV. Yet this ride, this was something off the charts. This was life changing. Everything was gone. He marveled that he had owned the Triumph for three years and only put 8,000 miles on it. That was going to change, he vowed.

He stopped and ate dinner in a tiny town whose name he forgot as soon as he left, and then had to force himself to be more alert in the encroaching darkness. This was the land where the deer and the antelope play, and sometimes they play at night. Striking one at speed would be almost certain death and he was glad he was less than 100 miles from home. Home... that word again. His trailer, parked on the land of his employer. That was...home? He wrestled with the idea as he rode through the darkness. The traditional view on home was a place you'd lived forever, knew everyone, knew every detail about your surroundings and everyone in it. Like Ruby and her diner there in Hulett. No doubt at all this area was home for Mel, was this home? Working a laborer's wage, living in his travel trailer, that didn't fit the definition at all. Still, there was Lester, his first real friend and an older man whom he could look up to and seek advice. Honest advice from an unassuming, honest man. And Terri, for all her defenses and aloofness, was honest, wasn't she? For all he knew, the answer was yes, but she was difficult to read and sometimes temperamental. Was she a friend? Could she be, while also being his employer? It was a nagging question. And what about that night by the tractor, when they looked at each other without interruption for a few seconds and the kiss on the tilt-o-whirl at the fair? Was there a "there" there? Logically, he thought no, but there was something in her eyes he could not dismiss. Suddenly this very simple life of a ranch laborer felt a tad more complicated than he'd bargained for.

He was only 20 miles from Alva and eager to get back. So he rolled on the throttle a little heavier than usual, and more than he should have in the darkness. From nowhere, red and blue lights materialized in his rear view mirrors.

"Damn! Really?" he cursed at himself inside the helmet as he pulled over. To his annoyance, the officer did not shut off the red and blue lights on the roof of the cruiser even after they'd stopped on the shoulder. In his left mirror, he saw the silhouette of the big cop walking toward him and then could only hang his head when the cop stood beside him. "Good evening Sheriff Peterson."

The big, uniformed man looked down at him, not making any recognizance of the helmeted rider. "License and registration please."

"Of course," Mel said as he removed his wallet, retrieving both documents and handing them over.

"Dominic Melvin Hatcher…" he began, and then stopped, looking up at the stars in the Wyoming sky. "Remove your helmet please." Mel complied. "Mr Hatcher," the big cop could hardly keep from laughing, "Could you explain to me please why it is that in such a small, rural area, you and I only meet on the side of the road when I am on duty?"

"Uhhh, I got nothing Dean. I mean, Sheriff Peterson."

"Son, you were going 80 miles per hour in a 55 zone, at night. Explain that to me."

"Umm, went to Sturgis, took the scenic route back, in a hurry to get home, I guess. That's all I got. No excuses."

The Sheriff let out a big exhale. "Ruby told me what you done in her diner, that morning when Dylan Turner confronted you. She said you let him be the big man instead of trashing her place. Is that so?"

125

"I guess."

"No, you don't guess, Mr Hatcher. Is that what happened?"

"Yes sir. He was looking to provoke something. I was up for it, but decided to back down so we didn't trash her place in the process. She seems really nice. I didn't want to do that to her, my first day in town and all."

"Uh huh… and you ain't afraid of taking on one Dylan Turner are you?"

"Why would you say that?"

He laughed, "I'm asking the questions here, son."

"Well, no sir. I'm not afraid of Mr Turner."

"I figured as much." He let out another long sigh, then he handed back the license and registration. "Slow your ass down. You seem like an OK guy to me, but this… this… motorcycle will get you killed out here. I found a guy out here two years ago on a bike that had run into a deer. You don't wanna know what he looked like. Don't be that guy."

"No sir," Mel responded earnestly. "I'll slow it down."

"Do that," and he surprised Mel by patting him on the shoulder before walking back to his cruiser.

Mel snicked the Triumph into gear and rolled back onto the road. He was surprised to see the police cruiser not behind him, but in fact had yanked a u-turn and gone the opposite direction. He rolled along at an easy pace, as he promised, and turned into the driveway only 20 minutes later. He rolled quietly past

Terri's house, noticing that her little Toyota was there, so he didn't want to wake her if she was already sleeping. As he rolled past the corner of the house that contained the office, he noticed a faint flicker from within, apparently the light from a TV or a computer monitor. Then he saw the silhouette of her head as she peered out the window. When he stopped the bike next to his trailer he looked down into the mirrors and could see she was still looking out the window at him. A smile crossed his face and he reached a decision.

I Ran to Alva

The Turn

The three were done with their morning strategy session and their coffee cups were all dry, so it was time to get started. But…

"Mel," Terri asked, "do you have any plans for Labor Day weekend?"

"Not really – why do you ask?" In the back of his mind, he was hoping that maybe she was beginning to think things through. It had been an uneasy time between them since the kiss at the fair. He wasn't giving up, but she hadn't shown any signs of opening up, either.

"Well, I have a favor to ask. And you can say no if you have to or if…"

"Just ask. The more words you speak to someone when they know you're going to ask them something, the more time you give them to think of a reason to say no. Just ask."

"A few of my 4-H girls want to enter their horses in the Labor Day Weekend competitions over at Belle Fourche. The girl whose father normally trailers the horses over there can't because his truck just broke down and he won't be able to have it fixed in time."

"Yes, we can use my truck."

"Really? You mean it?"

128

"No. Now that you asked me a second time, I take it all back. I'd rather set fire to it than use it to help you in any way."

Though his face was expressionless and his voice was Ben Stein flat, she knew he was kidding and a giggle escaped her lips. He sure could be charming. "Thank you."

"When, where, how long?"

"Uh, that Friday afternoon the truck needs to be at their place probably by 3PM. Her dad will help you hook up their trailer and he will do all the other work, loading everything. You don't have to do a thing."

"Uhhhhhhh huh," he teased.

"Once the horses and gear are loaded, you just drive to the grounds at Belle Fourche. They will unload and drop the trailer there. Then you can come back that Monday about 1PM for the return trip. And you will be paid your regular pay plus 25 cents a mile."

"They're actually going to pay me mileage?" He seemed surprised.

"No, I am."

"Forget it. I'll accept the hourly wage but not the mileage."

"What?"

"You started this conversation asking me for a favor. And I granted it. I'm willing to accept pay for my time because I'll be doing it during hours I would have normally been working, but if I charge you every last penny of expenses it won't be a favor, will it? Just...pay for work."

"I was just trying to be fair to you."

"You're just trying to be formal to me."

She understood his perspective, even if he was wrong, but he had a point as to how it looked. "You're right...fine... hourly pay only then. And thank you," she concluded, squeezing his hand briefly.

For a moment, she let him look into those eyes again, but only for a moment. And it frustrated him. He could see it. He could *see* that she had feelings for him, he could feel it. Dammit, what was her problem? The few weeks he'd been trying to be patient and bide his time was starting feel like years. And even though Lester had the good manners not to ask, he knew that the older man knew what was up. It was like the biggest open-but-unspoken secret between them all. Fortunately, they were all very busy indeed with their daily lives, leaving little time to ruminate on the situation.

The few days passed and on that Friday, Terri rode with Mel in the big Ford diesel over to the horse and trailer pickup. She introduced Mel to her 4-H girl Sarah and her parents, Doug and Molly. Mel and Doug chatted briefly and then walked over to where the trailer was parked. As Doug described what he thought would work for the hookup and then loading the horses, Mel could tell the man had experience, so decided just to follow his lead. The hookup took only a couple minutes and Doug's expertise at trailer-loading horses made that task a breeze. Mel helped Doug load all the plastic bins of tack as well as a couple bales of hay and a small bag of grain, which they accomplished in less than a half hour. A quick double check of the trailer lights and electric brakes and they were ready to roll. The trip would probably only take a little over an hour, but Mel was looking forward to having Terri in the truck all that time. Not that he was going to push, but just enjoyed talking with her, especially when it was just them.

The ride over was less relaxing than they had hoped. The infamous winds of Wyoming were making their presence known, trying to push the truck and trailer anywhere except where Mel wanted them to go. Terri was impressed with Mel's ability to handle it all without seeming stressed. He certainly kept his eyes open and a sure grip on the steering wheel, but was calm as could be. They managed some conversation and she was relieved that it didn't focus on "them." That was nice of him, she thought. She knew it was on his mind, she could see it in his eyes whenever he looked at her, but being confined like this, just the two of them, could be unbearable if he had to go there. Mostly, they talked about building the little bridge across the creek and what a score it was to find all that lumber for the project. They also talked about the coming weekend and what she and her 4-H girls were going to do the whole time. It sounded to Mel like Terri was really going to have fun and he was glad for her, she deserved it.

"What are you going to do all weekend Mel?"

"Oh, I thought of taking the ATV to a couple spots I've been reading about."

"Maybe you should hook up with Lester and go fishing or something."

"Maybe, but not likely. It's best for two men who work together to have a day off from each other, too. That's what my Grampa always said anyway."

"Sure, I understand."

"Sooooo, I dunno, I will probably take the ATV out, like I said, go camping. That sort of thing."

They pulled onto the grounds at Belle Fourche where the Events Director met them at the gate and instructed them on unloading the horses and then where to park the trailer. The Director was a tall blonde female about Mel's age and she made no secret of admiring his arm resting on the truck's door sill. Her smile and the way she drew out certain words as she talked to him were so obvious, even Mel himself picked up on the vibe. And he smiled, too, not so much smiling back at her, but wondering and pretty much knowing that Terri would also perceive the Director's personal, friendly demeanor. He could hardly keep from laughing when he heard Terri huff once, but he decided not to push it, so he bid the Director adieu and rolled the truck and trailer to the designated spot.

"Well, she was really nice," he observed flatly.

"If you say so," Terri replied with ice in her words.

He couldn't keep from laughing. And she couldn't pretend not to know what he was laughing about. The Director's flirtation was so obvious that Mel had to know that she noticed it. And try as she might, she could not talk herself out of feeling it and could not make herself behave as if it had not happened. She had to come to terms with the reality of her attraction for him, but before that could move forward, she'd have to reveal everything and then let him decide. But he deserved to make an informed choice, she owed him that much. She was utterly certain what his choice would be, and she would never ever hold it against him, but at least then the tension and the uncertainty would be gone, even if that meant he would be gone. Yet she felt that he had to know and so she decided she would tell him next week. She would tell him why she ran from her past and why she ran to Alva. So right now, this moment, she thought would be the last time he'd see her as he believed her to be, and she did so love the way he looked at her.

Doug, his daughter Sarah and a few others had convoyed in separate cars ahead of Mel and Terri and were waiting to unload everything when they got there. Doug had high praise for Mel's ability to handle the rig under the windy conditions and the two men engaged in amiable chat as they went about their work.

"You know," Doug said, "if you're not real busy, you should hang around here this weekend. You could spend more time with Terri and maybe enjoy some of the competitions. And the motel made me take a room with two beds, so you could use one of them instead of driving back and forth."

"What about Sarah? Or your wife?"

"Sarah's staying in one room with all the girls and Molly is only coming up for the day on Sunday. Her dad is ill, so she's spending time with him."

"Hmmm," Mel thought out loud, "that is a very generous offer, Doug. Not sure if I will take you up on it yet, but I do appreciate it. Let's do this… let's exchange phone numbers and I will get in touch with you if I decide to come back. Is that cool?"

"Of course, no worries."

So they exchanged information and Mel looked around for Terri, just to say goodbye or something, but didn't see her anywhere. That was disappointing, but he knew she probably had a lot to get organized. He would have liked to say goodbye, but he hopped up into the crew cab, lit the diesel's fire and rolled out. Terri emerged from the stable where they had put the horses just in time to see his truck drive out the exit gate. Her heart sunk and she felt a little sick. She saw a utility shed with an open door and made a bee line for it. Once inside, she sat down on an overturned bucket and sobbed. It was probably ten minutes before she composed herself enough to walk out and face the world again. Sarah saw her first and noticed her red and puffy eyes.

"What's wrong Miss Terri? Are you OK?"

"Yes, Sarah, I'll be fine. Just worried about my uncle in Billings, the one I've told you girls about," she lied.

"Ohhhhhh….I'm sorry Miss Terri. I'm really sorry" and she hugged her tightly.

Terri stroked the top of her head and returned the hug. "Thank you, sweety. I'll be OK. I'll be OK."

Sarah looked up at her and smiled, "Sure?"

"Yes…now let's start our big girls' weekend on a high note and have us some fun, yeah? No troubles, no boys, none of that. Just us girls and our horses!"

Sarah laughed and they exchanged a playful fist bump and turned toward the stable to catch up with the rest of the girls and get the weekend rolling.

Mel's drive home was somber. Alone and left to his thoughts, he pitched back and forth between telling himself to forget all about Terri and move on, to devising schemes to make her open up. In the end, he knew that she was a strong woman and would never be rushed into anything she didn't want. So, as it had been since the county fair, the burden was still on him to wait. And the burden of the decision…how long to wait…was also completely on him. He hated that. He hated the idea that he might decide one day to just throw in the towel, one day too soon. That if he had waited one more day, his patience would have been rewarded. That was the damned awful truth, wasn't it? How would he know the difference between being patient and just spinning his wheels? The questions, the doubts and the second guessing were driving him nuts.

When he got back home he decided to go on the internet to check out those ATV trails again and make a plan for his weekend. Then he got to thinking about Doug's offer and he began to wonder if maybe the area around Belle Fourche had anything to offer for exploring with an ATV. Within an hour, he saw that indeed there was, so he decided to alter his plans. He finished eating the small pizza he had picked up on the way home and washed it down with his second beer. Then he called Doug to see if he was cool with the plan. To his relief, Doug was still extending the offer and looked forward to seeing him.

Doug teased him, though, said a very pretty and tall blond had asked about him. Mel laughed and thanked him for letting him know.

Then he opened Pandora on his computer and plugged the amplifier cord into the computer so he could hear the music through the trailer's very powerful speakers. As he was deciding which of his "stations" to listen to while he prepared everything for the weekend, he felt like he needed something to soothe his nerves over Terri, so he chose the Enya station. He wondered if any guys his age, guys that were anything like him, also listened to Enya. He smiled at the thought, probably more male listeners than most people might think, but it would be one those deals where no "real man" could admit it. The first song "Pilgrim" came on and he turned it up quite loud. He'd heard the song many times and was fond of it because it reminded him of his deceased uncle, the so-called black sheep of his mother's family. He was a poor soul born perhaps at the wrong time in history and just lacked a little control over his appetites and impulses. Yet he had always been good to Mel and kind, too. As with many people who lived life as the uncle did, he died young. At the funeral, most people whispered to themselves about what a tragedy and what a waste his life had been and how sad it all was. Even his own sister, Mel's mom, spoke the same way. It was disturbing to him that he, at the tender age of 20, was the only one at the funeral to shed a tear for the man. He stood very still for the duration of "Pilgrim" and delved into pleasant thoughts and memories of his uncle. When it ended, he reluctantly began moving to get everything ready for the weekend.

The next morning he had the ATV loaded and was rolling east before 6am. He reached the National Forest north of Belle Fourche area by 7:30 and was exploring by 8:00. The maps, plus his GPS, were absolutely accurate and he had a great time going from one point of interest to another via trails and fire roads really not great to drive with a regular truck. It was 4PM by the time he'd completed the planned loop and he was ready for dinner and a shower. He loaded up the ATV into the Ford's spacious bed and headed for Doug's motel. On the drive there, he called him to confirm that he was on his way.

"Hey, your timing will be good," Doug said.

"How do you mean?"

"Well, a few of us grown ups are going to dinner and then heading over to a bar we know, for a few drinks. Nothing elaborate, just a break for the adults."

"Well, that's sounds good and all, but…"

"Terri's going too." He added quickly.

"Umm, yeah, well, I guess that's OK, that's fine," he stammered as he tried to sound disinterested.

Doug laughed, "C'mon dude….you ain't fooling me."

"Mel let out an audible sigh, "But it's complicated."

"It always is. Don't sweat it. Just get on down here and get cleaned up. You should have plenty of time. I won't tell Terri you're coming; it'll be a nice surprise."

"Allright, see ya then."

So he ended the call and simply tried not to over think the whole situation as he drove south. He arrived at the motel, found Doug's room and dragged all of his gear from the truck inside. Doug had left a note with the name of the restaurant and some simple directions, so Mel folded it up and set it next to his wallet on the night stand. He shaved, took a quick shower and headed out. Belle Fourche is not an overly large town, so he had little trouble finding the restaurant. When he went in, he saw the group sitting near the back and Terri saw him immediately. She waved and flashed a very big smile. It was a surprise, but a good one. At the table, she scooted over her position at the large group booth so Mel could sit next to her. He'd have expected it if it was just her, Lester and him, but didn't expect her to make such an obvious gesture in front of others. It pleased him.

During dinner, they shared their experiences and observations of how all the girls did during the day. The stories were both funny and charming to Mel and he half-wished he'd been around to see them. Terri and the others were equally interested in his off road excursion and he showed them some pictures he'd taken on his iPhone and would download later. After dinner, they all decided to head over to the bar Doug had mentioned. It was actually owned by the brother of one of the ladies in their group. That sounded promising, Mel thought, as he didn't have a high opinion of most bars and generally avoided them. Mel offered Terri a ride and she accepted. Her mood on the short ride to the bar was decidedly upbeat but they didn't talk about anything of personal significance.

The bar was already about 2/3 full when they arrived, as it was well known that one of the premier bands in the area was going to be playing. It was a nice mix of a crowd, early 20's to late 40's, mostly jeans and cowboy hats, but a noticeable mix of urban dress code, too. As they were making their way to a couple adjacent tables, Mel spotted Dylan Turner off in the distance. At first, it surprised him, but then he remembered the family's saw mill was actually about halfway between Alva and here, so he was probably somewhat of a local. He wondered if Dylan would put someone else in their place tonight after a few beers. He hoped not, it just seemed so ridiculous. As he watched Dylan, though, he appeared to be in an easy going mood and real loose.

The group all got seated and ordered their first round of drinks. Mel laughed at Terri when she ordered a chocolate martini. "You're so….cosmopolitan," he laughed.

"You have nothing to laugh about. Let's see, what on earth might Mel possibly order?" she asked in mockery. "Hey, I'll take a wild guess, go way out on a limb here and say you're gonna order a stout - the beer that looks like maple syrup."

The whole table was quite amused at their banter. Doug just smiled at Mel and looked away. Mel knew what he was thinking.

"Good guess," he replied to Terri, "but at least I don't have to tell the waitress how the drink is made. What makes you think it'll be done right anyway?"

"I'll take my chances. I'm not afraid to step out of my comfort zone."

"Not with drinks, anyway," he said to her, as quietly as he could.

"Could we not do this right here?"

"I'm sorry," he said sincerely. "I didn't mean to."

She bumped her shoulder into his as a sign of accepting his apology and he was grateful she let him off the hook. She was right. Even though they had a lot to discuss, this was not the time or place. Mel excused himself to find the men's room. On his way there, Dylan recognized him, smiled and walked over to shake his hand. Mel was quite surprised, and relieved, but Dylan was, what – relaxed? He seemed jovial.

"Did you manage to get that front drive shaft fixed?" he asked, recalling the experience at the mill.

"Oh, yeah, sure did. That trick you did with the plug worked great, I really appreciated that."

"No sweat man, glad it worked out." But then he looked at Mel with a sort of hesitation on his face. "Hey man…..uhhhhhh, I just want to say thanks, you know, for not saying nothin'. You know, about that day in the barn when we tangled."

Mel just shrugged, "Well, yeah, dude, I mean I told ya that was between us. Nobody had to know."

"Yeah, but truth is…around here…. People, some people, don't like me so much. For them, news of me coming out on the short end of a deal like that would spread like a wildfire."

"Well, you and I really didn't have a history, Dylan. I have no idea how long I will ultimately live in this area, but for as long as it is, I just want to try and get along with people as best I can. To go around talking about something like that…I

140

mean….who's gonna want to become my friend or have anything to do with me if I'm…"

"Like me…" Dylan said, finishing the sentence that Mel started but then tried to drop.

"I didn't mean it like that."

"No, no, I believe you, but actually, that is the truth. I have been an asshole. You know, I was a big shot football player around here in high school, got a full ride to Montana State."

"Yes, I heard."

"But then flunked out my freshman year. Came back here and everybody and their brother did nothing but mock me. I was a joke. I mean, what the hell did I know about college and stuff? Parties, pussy everywhere, and no one telling me that I was actually going to have to crack the books. Not like high school where they let me slide because I made the school look good."

"That's actually a pretty common story for high school athletes, unfortunately."

"Yeah…so I come back here…a big joke…19 years old, dumb as a fence post, no other school will touch me because of my grades, lucky to have the piss-ant job I got at the family's mill."

"I can see how you'd have a chip on your shoulder, Dylan, but we've all been kicked. At some point, some point, you just have to let that crap go. Look, I barely know ya, I'm not gonna tell you how to live or anything. Just try to understand we've all been kicked. We've all been given a bad hand at some point in life. Like my Grandpa used to ask me, "What are you gonna do? Are you gonna let that one thing ruin the rest of your life?"

Dylan just smiled, but Mel could see the gears were turning. Could be that maybe Mr Turner wasn't bad to the bone as so many made him out to be. And just maybe… this community helped to *create* the monster they now feared. That was an interesting thought. Mel turned to look back at his table and could see Terri staring at them with a very anxious look on her face. He knew it was time to finish the business he started to do and get back over there. "Well, I gotta duck into the head and then get back over to my table there. Hope I'll see ya around sometime, huh?" he concluded with a smile and they shook hands again.

"For sure, dude. Have a good one," and Dylan returned the smile.

Back at the table, Mel knew Terri was going to pepper him with questions. She didn't waste any time.

"Do I need my eyes checked? Were you playing nice with Dylan?"

"Sure," he shrugged as if it was nothing, but he was aware of the entire table listening to this conversation. They all knew, or knew of, Dylan and were stunned to see an apparently nice guy like Mel carrying on such a friendly conversation with him, especially in light of what happened in Ruby's place his first day in town. By now, the story had 10 different variations, but they all had one thing in common – that Dylan had bullied yet another man in town and the man had backed down. And they knew that man was Mel. So the group had a keen interest in this turn of events.

"What did you guys talk about?"

"History, basically."

"History?"

"Yeah. His. I understand him now."

"In a three minute conversation, you understand what makes him tick?"

"Yep. Because he wanted it. He wanted someone to hear it, to hear why he thinks and acts the way he does."

"Which is...?"

"I don't think it would be right to say. It was a private conversation, personal stuff."

She searched his eyes for that little twinkle that would reveal he was just playing around, but it wasn't there. He was serious. This was a bit much to comprehend. The rest of the table was on the same page as Terri. They wanted to press Mel further, but they didn't know him well enough.

Doug, on the other hand, thought the whole thing was quite cool. He had also been watching Mel talk with Dylan and saw the easy manner with which Mel conducted himself around the larger man with the fierce reputation. Mel was not at all intimidated; Doug could see it in his body language. On the other hand, Doug had noticed that when Mel was speaking to Dylan, there were a couple times Dylan stared intently at the floor, like a student accepting a lesson from a teacher. And suddenly, Doug understood something. That Dylan perceived Mel as a peer, as an equal. And if that was true, then yes, it was entirely likely that he might have revealed personal history to him. Doug knew that people feel closest to people whom they deem their equals and will often confide in them. Dylan had always s made it known that no man around here was his equal, hadn't he? He'd made that clear on several occasions, but Doug saw with his own eyes that Dylan did indeed accept Mel as his equal. He proved it with his actions and his willingness to engage in a personal conversation. Of course that made Doug wonder a little about Mel.

Eventually, the group and even Terri stopped pressing Mel about the details of his chat with Dylan and they all began to enjoy the band. They took their turns at dancing and people watching and all the normal things people do in a bar on Saturday night.

During one of the band's breaks, they became aware of a ruckus at the far end of the bar near the pool tables. "What did that asshole start this time?" Terri asked out loud, as she saw Dylan. He was backed against the bar, and two men approximately his size were having a very intense conversation with him and it was obvious they were demanding him to step outside. Didn't seem fair, for sure, two of them, but sometimes two men who've been pushed around will team up against their oppressor. Terri thought if he got his ass beat, it might teach him a lesson. About the time she turned to make a comment to Mel, she noticed he was already up and walking quickly in the direction of the three men. "What the hell?" she practically screamed. The rest of the group saw him, too and looked rapidly at each other, hoping the other had an answer or a clue.

"Who are your friends, Dylan?" Mel said loudly, standing behind the two men.

"Uhh, hey Mel…these guys…"

"It ain't none of your damn business," one of the men practically spit the words through clenched teeth.

"Sure it is. Two on one, that makes it everybody's business, because that isn't a fight – it's assault."

"Oohhhhhh……..uuuhhhhhhhh" the second man stammered. "Hey, it's you" he said looking at Mel. The look on his face was a comical combination of recognition, admiration and fear. The second man said to the first man, "It's him, dude, it's the Hatchet. It's Dom Hatcher."

The second man recognized him also and his face revealed the same thoughts as his partner. "OK, look Mr. Hatcher; we got no business with you. Hell, we're both fans of yours, but this guy here…" he said referring back to Dylan. "This guy's had an ass beating coming for a long time now."

"OK," Mel said, "So the two of you draw straws and decide which one of you is going to do it." Mel had his chin up just enough to show that he meant business. "Because, as I said, two on one is assault."

The two men looked at each other, realizing that whichever one of them did not take on Dylan was probably going to have to take on The Hatchet. And neither one wanted that. This plan was unraveling quickly. Dylan was no longer standing defensively against the bar, but was now standing squared up to the men. Yet he was also confused. These two guys, whom Dylan had known for a decade or more, instantly backed down when they saw Mel, but they didn't call him Mel. The "Hatchet"? What the hell was that all about? Well, he'd figure that out later But this might be a good time to straighten out the problem that started all this.

"Darby," Dylan said to the first man, "I know what this is about, and you got it wrong."

"Like hell I do." He replied, moving nearer toward Dylan, putting the two men face to face. "You beat the shit out of my 17 year old cousin, for what? For WHAT??!!!"

"Because he was trying to rape that girl he was with, Darby. That's the truth."

"Bullshit! Bullshit! You lying bastard!"

Mel kept a close eye on the second man as Dylan and Darby got more intense. There was now a crowd gathered round and half a dozen people had their cell phones out, either on the phone with 9-1-1 or maybe just calling their friends to tell them about the show down.

"Darby... you know Sheriff Peterson was called. And you know he's a hardass and you should know he doesn't think much of me. He wouldn't hesitate to arrest me for punching out a minor. So why didn't he?"

"Because you threatened him that you'd beat his ass if he said anything!"

"No I didn't. Your cousin knew that Peterson would arrest *him* if he knew the whole truth. So your cousin promised me he'd never touch that girl again, or any girl. He told Peterson that he'd been drinking and attacked me, so I hit him in self defense. Peterson bought it, or at least appeared to, but you're right about one thing; I did tell your cousin if he ever touched another girl, that I would find him and finish the ass beating he deserved."

Darby stood quietly, still angry, but uncertain what to think. When he looked into Dylan's eyes, there was no doubt, no hesitation, he gave no indication at all that he was lying. And what he said about Peterson was true, every word. Peterson would have loved to arrest him, but didn't. Maybe, maybe Dylan was telling the truth. That didn't make sense, either, but he had nothing else to go on. And he sure as hell couldn't take him now solo, could he? What a suck situation, he thought. "Allright Turner, I'm gonna let this go for now, but if you're lying, I'll find out. And if it comes to that, I'll have 5 guys with me just in case you have The Hatchet on your hip again," he finished, looking at Mel. "Hatchet… you have lousy taste in friends. Come on," he said to the first man, "let's get out of here."

The two pushed their way out of the crowd around them and hustled out the door. No doubt the cops would be here any time. They could always work on their alibi later.

"Thanks man." Dylan said to Mel. "I owe ya."

"This is what happens, Dylan,"Mel said bluntly, showing no signs of friendship. "This is what happens when you bully and beat people down. Pretty soon, they team up and they'll beat you down. And they'll just *keep* beating you down. I hope everything you said was true. It would be nice to think you used your fists for something good, but did you notice he didn't believe you? Do you think anyone standing within earshot believed you? Probably not. Why? Because of your reputation.'

Dylan stood quietly and absorbed the lecture, knowing Mel was right. "I'm...you're right dude... I'm sorry...but that situation... I told the truth and he'll find that out. He will."

"So what? Will he walk up to you, apologize and beg your forgiveness? No! He'll still think you're as big of a jerk as he ever did – maybe just not a liar, is all, but he still won't like you. He will still resent you for years of your behavior."

Dylan shrugged and looked at the floor. "I'm sorry for putting you in that situation, but thank you for backing me up. And I'm sorry, Mel, I am really sorry for that day in Ruby's. I'm sorry."

Now Mel was starting to feel bad, he was not comfortable lecturing and reprimanding people. "Well, this situation here, no reason to apologize, OK, that was chicken shit, what they were trying to do. Trying to double up on you – it was chicken shit, but dammit, man...think! Think about what you're doing. Just... think...dammit...."

"OK, yeah, I will. I get it. Mel...what was that they called you? The Hatchet? What was that? How did they know you?"

"From a past life I am trying to forget. I gotta get back to my table." He concluded, but patted Dylan on the shoulder before turning away.

"So," Terri started as soon as Mel returned to the table, "help us understand what we all just saw. The bully of northern Wyoming – that would be Dylan – was about to get the ass beating he so richly deserved," she paused with a raise of her eyebrows, "but you stepped in to back him up. You. One of his earlier…victims. Yeah, I know about the morning in Ruby's."

Mel was visibly surprised. He didn't know she knew about that. She had never mentioned it, but he knew that Lester seemed to know everyone and everything and he was betting he'd told her.

"So you… of all people…step in to back him up. What the hell is wrong with this picture?"

Mel was aware that the whole table was staring at him. "Two men on one is never right. It is never right. I heard those men say why they were confronting Dylan, but he was able to explain to them why they were wrong. They would have beaten him for no reason."

"Big deal," she said. "He had it coming for a dozen *other* reasons, so what if it was the wrong one?"

"I'm really sorry to hear you say that. There are a lot of people that need forgiveness, for a whole host of reasons. The conversation I had with him earlier, the one you asked about, I think he is thinking about his life and his behavior. If he changes, I hope people could forgive him. We all need forgiveness for something. Well, maybe not all of us," he said, staring straight in to her eyes. "Some of us haven't lived by the straight and narrow, so maybe we hope that those who have can one day forgive us." At that, he stood. "I'm going back to

149

the motel, Doug, but I won't be staying tonight. I'll be getting my stuff and I'll see you all Monday." And he walked out, leaving them all speechless.

Terri looked around at the table, wondering if anyone's eyes held a clue about what she should think or do, but they only looked away in awkward silence. Finally Doug spoke.

"There was a hidden message in there Terri," he said slowly. "I don't know what it is, I've never really talked with Mel, but his reaction to you was really because of what he said about Dylan. Mel thinks he sees a possibility that Dylan might change, that is what he said, right?"

Terri nodded.

"So Dylan would need to be forgiven, wouldn't he? But why would Mel get upset over the possibility that you might not forgive Dylan? On the face of it, whether or not you could forgive Dylan is irrelevant, but what you said to him indicated that you might not be able to forgive, period. So what would that mean to him... if... *he* needed to be forgiven for something?"

"But he's never done or said anything to me."

"Maybe not you, but maybe he did something else he needs to be forgiven for. And you just demonstrated that you do not extend forgiveness easily."

It began to sink in. Doug was right. Painfully right. What message had she just sent him? And she, of all people, needed forgiveness didn't she? Maybe soon, she would actually need it from Mel. What had she done? The answer, if there was one coming, would have to wait until at least Monday.

I Ran to Alva

Baring it All

Terri saw Mel's truck pull into the loading area promptly at one o'clock. She watched from a distance as he greeted Doug. The two men talked briefly and went about hooking up the trailer, loading the horses and all the tack and gear they had brought. All the girls got situated with the cars they were riding in and Terri momentarily considered asking one of them for a ride, but she knew she was just being chicken, afraid to face Mel for the ride home. Afraid to talk to him. She'd had all weekend to think about what she said, what Doug said and the tacit message she must have sent to Mel. She had to let him know that was not her. She had to find a way to tell or demonstrate that if he felt there was something in his past to be forgiven, then she could.

"Hey, Terri, I was wondering where you were." He greeted her with a warm smile. It surprised her.

"Umm, well I was helping some of the girls double check their stuff, making sure no one forgot anything," she lied, and not too convincingly.

"Allright, well, you ready to go?"

"Sure." They both got in the big Ford and, after a brief systems check, Mel put it in gear and rolled out, cognizant of all the cars convoying behind him. They were barely 2 miles down the road when Terri could no longer contain her thoughts. "Mel, what I said in the bar the other night, about Dylan. I was wrong. I shouldn't have said that."

"No worries. What you said was true. People have done all kinds of bad things to others. So even if they don't get what was coming to 'em at the hands of someone they actually wronged, it's OK. It's like a universal justice, yes? Even if you're inclined to forgive them because they did nothing to you, they still deserve to be punished because they wronged somebody somewhere."

She was stunned by his words. And even more stunned because it wasn't that he was speaking something of which he was simply wrong and ignorant. She knew, she could sense that he really didn't believe what he was saying. He was just being vindictive, trying to make a point of some sort, but she understood.

"Stop it Mel. Just stop it. I don't believe that, and I don't think you believe it either."

"Oh, so now you're going to tell me I am wrong *and* I don't really know what I say I know. This just gets better by the mile. Please keep talking because I am so charmed by your analysis of my motives and personality." His voice was beginning to betray the calm façade.

"No Mel! Stop it!" her voice cracked, "I was wrong what I said the other night. Yes, I despise Dylan, but I was wrong when I said he didn't deserve forgiveness. I was wrong to say it because that is not truly how I feel. It isn't."

"I don't know," he countered, "you seemed pretty resolute the other night."

"No…no. I was confused… that you defended him. For a minute, I found myself doubting you. I let myself think for a moment that you saw some sort of sympathy toward him because maybe you were like him. That you saw a sort kindred spirit you could befriend."

"Are you out of your mind? Do you honestly think…?"

"NO!" she cut him off "You *aren't* like him, Mel. I don't think that, but I was confused for just a moment that night. Haven't you ever been confused and made the wrong conclusion about someone?"

Her words went like a dagger into the soft spot, as he thought immediately of Phillip and all the wrong things he'd thought about him. It gave him to pause, so he slowed his mind down and listened to her. "Well, yes, OK, I have."

"That's all it was, just a moment where I misunderstood. And it confused me. I was confused, that's all."

"So, OK… fine," he allowed. "Why are we talking about this? What does what happened in the bar have to do with anything? Help me connect the dots. Why is forgiving Dylan Turner suddenly such a big deal?"

"It isn't, but…" she hesitated, "forgiving me is, or might be, a very big deal."

"OK, fine, I forgive you, it's done." He said, not grasping where she was going.

"No, Mel. It isn't done." She took his hand and held it. She looked down at the floor to gather her thoughts. "I am very fond of you, Mel. More than I am prepared to say right now. More than I dare say right now." And he saw the tears streaming down her cheeks as she kept her eyes shut tight. "When we kissed at the fair that night, and all the other times when you have looked at me – I know you could see how I feel Mel. I'm not a great poker player, I can't fake very well. I am drawn to you at least as much as you are to me. I've kept you at a distance for a very valid reason, a reason…"

"Are you married? Is there…?"

"No no… nothing like that, but I will tell you later, after we get home."

"Why not now?"

"Because this is… pretty big… and it ties into what we've been talking about with respect to forgiveness. You will have to decide if you can forgive me. For you to do that, you will have to understand the full scope of what I am talking about. I can't tell you verbally. I will just have to show you. And then you will have to decide. I want you to know that I will understand and respect your decision, no matter what it is."

His head was swimming with confusion. She was basically confessing…what? That she... loved him? Did she? Is that what she implied? Did he love her? Had it gone that far already? What the hell could possibly be so awful to stand in the way of that? Why couldn't she at least divulge some of it now? But he sensed the trembling in her hand and her tears persisted. Pressing her now would do no good. Maybe he could show some good will at this moment by just waiting on her, waiting for when they'd get home and she could tell him everything. Luckily, it wasn't a very long drive.

When they arrived at Doug's house, Terri stayed in the truck and asked Mel to tell everyone she'd gotten motion sick, or to make up some other white lie so she wouldn't have to talk to anyone. Doug was not fooled.

"Whatever you talked about, Mel, take a deep breath before you react. Let it sink in and just let it sit there a while before you decide anything."

Mel appreciated Doug's calm demeanor. He guessed Doug to be about 15 years older and clearly the man had taken notes of his life experiences because not once in their few exchanges had Mel regarded him as anything less than wise. From trailering horses to personal relationships, Doug had paid attention along his path in life.

"Well, I don't really know what is yet to come," he replied. Yeah, we talked on the drive and she hinted at something she still has to tell me, but I don't know what it is. We ironed out what happened the other night and I'm cool with it, but I guess there's still more."

"OK, well… just remember the full perspective of what happened the other night. It seems you are willing to forgive Dylan of his past transgressions if he puts his past behind him. Can you extend that same indulgence to her?"

"Yeah of course," he said instantly, "what can be so bad? I mean it's Terri. Did she get arrested for shop lifting when she was 16? She cheated on her merit badge tests when she was a girl scout and so she volunteers now with 4-H to assuage her guilt? I mean, come on."

Doug chuckled a little, but still he kept Mel on point. "You don't know Mel. If she is upset about it, maybe you should prepare for the worst. That way, your head will be clear when you have to decide what you're going to do, but whatever that is make an honest choice. Be honest and ultimately, everyone will understand your choice."

"Straight up," was Mel's simple reply. The two men shook hands in a far more friendly and brotherly way than they had before. Mel found himself thinking that he hoped he and Doug would bump into each other now and again. The man was not robust and outdoorsy, he even dressed a little bit preppy, but he was sincere, unassuming and pretty damn smart. Mel got back into his truck where Terri waited silently and they headed for home. She didn't reach for his hand and she didn't say anything, but merely looked at him briefly when he got in and then stared back out the window again as they left. She finally spoke when they got in the driveway.

"Drop me at the house. Give me an hour or so and then I'll call you to come over, OK?"

He merely nodded and she squeezed his hand briefly before getting out. He watched her walk up the front porch stairs as though she was carrying an extra hundred pounds on her back. The gravity of the situation began to creep up on him. He had always been good at reading people's body English, and what he read in Terri made him feel instantly sad. The words he'd spoke to Doug regarding Terri and "how bad could it be" were swirling in his mind now and he had a sneaking suspicion they were about to bite him. He rolled the truck up to his place, went inside and took Doug's advice; he prepared for the worst. To kill some time, he made himself a little snack and then found he had no appetite. He mindlessly cleaned up a few things lying about and then went outside to tidy up around the trailer. He forced himself not to look at Terri's house, lest she might be looking out at him. Didn't want to put any pressure on her. Maybe if she saw him outside doing mundane things, then she'd be relaxed, believing that he was calm and casual. Back inside, he sat down to watch TV for a bit and then jumped when his phone rang. He answered and "Come on over now" was all she said.

He walked on "nervous knees" as his Grandpa used to say. Was there anything worse than anticipating something awful? But he bucked himself up, remembering that this was Terri, after all. And he cheered himself up, thinking that once he calmed her down and assured her that this, this "terrible thing" was nothing of the sort, they were going to move forward, yes? Isn't that what she had implied in the truck? That was good news. This was actually going to be a good thing. He didn't need to knock on the door as she was waiting for him. She took his hand and led him into the house without saying a word, but he noticed that her steps were unsteady and it occurred to him that her breath wreaked of liquor. She was drunk? That made no sense. She led him into the corner room where the computer and the large TV sat, and from where she could peer out at him and Lester as they did their work.

"Sit down in the chair," she said softly. "I have something you have to see and you have to know about." Her words were slightly slurred; she had clearly drunk quite a bit. That alone was a shock to Mel and he was filled with dread. "I want you to know that I am fond of you, Mel, but I have to be completely honest with you because we can never be anything if I am not totally open. I want to tell you now, in advance, that I never really was what you are about to learn. I lost myself for a while, a few years, but have found myself again. In this place, with you and with Lester and all these decent people around me, I found myself again. So try to remember that and think about it while you decide if you can forgive me."

He thought his heart would beat out of his chest as she reached forward and hit a button on the computer. The TV screen was sync'ed up to it and his eyes locked on. It was the beginning of a movie; a comically cheesy and cheap movie and there he saw Terri. She was a few years younger, her hair was longer and she was a good 15-20 pounds slimmer. Wow, did she look great in that bikini as she emerged from a swimming pool. Dang was she hot. And then it hit him… it was a porn movie. In short order he saw that she was the star, not a bit actor or a supporting role, but the star of the show. He watched long enough for the lead "actor" to completely undress her, hoping and denying that what he was seeing was not real and that at some point it would all just stop. Yet as the man on the screen began to perform his "role", he realized it was not going to stop and he'd seen enough porn movies in his life to know what followed. He switched off the computer and sat in silence. He was aware that she was still sitting on the couch behind him and he could hear her crying softly.

His gut reaction was not really even one of disgust or revulsion. After all, he had watched many such movies; they were widely viewed by men of his age. He had even met one female starlet of the adult film industry when in LA, and she wasn't vile or gross. If anything, his negative reaction to it seemed like it was…what? Simply practical. A regular guy just didn't date porn stars, and he was a regular guy.

"Ummm," he began awkwardly while he still stared at the blank screen. "How long ago was this?"

Through her tears, she managed to answer, "Right after I graduated college, so about 5 or 6 years ago."

"OK… are there more?"

"Yessss…" voice trailed off at a high pitch and her crying intensified.

"How many more?"

"F-f-f-f-f-ive."

With each answer, he felt his heart sink, but he wasn't angry. It was just shock. "How long has it been since you did the last one?"

"I did them all in 18 months…" she managed a breath, "so the last one was, I guess, at least 4 years ago."

"How did it start?"

"I majored in drama at Oregon." She paused to draw a breath and to take another drink of whiskey. "I moved to LA when I graduated, to get my acting career going. Long story short, one of the companies I auditioned for made porn movies, but I didn't know it at the time. The owner was wealthy, not even 30, charmed me and wined and dined me, I didn't know he was setting me up. Before I knew it, he had broken down all my inhibitions and convinced me I was a natural."

"Did you like it?"

"At first I did. It seemed exciting and rebellious and everywhere I went, people recognized me and treated me special. And I made a lot of money."

"How did it end?"

"I caught him giving a... so-called audition... to another young girl, and then I realized I was just part of the chain. I made the last two movies only for the money and then couldn't stand it anymore. I just felt so awful."

"Is that how you bought this place?"

"Mostly." She was surprised by Mel's calm demeanor and his reasonable questions that were free of accusations. She began to breathe just a little easier. "I left LA and moved to New York to start over. I managed to land some TV commercials and had a nice gig as a sportswear model until they found out about the porn. After word spread in New York, I was toast. So I realized my acting or modeling career was over, permanently. I was built up and then wrecked by all kinds of people who made a lot of money by building me up *and* by wrecking me, but I was lucky in one respect – my dad taught me to save my money. So I left New York literally on a whim. I just drove and drove and I went to visit my uncle in Billings. Stayed with him a couple weeks. Told him everything. He never told my parents. My dad's a rabbi in my hometown, can you believe that?"

"Wow!"

"Yeah, wow. The rabbi's girl turned whore. Anyway, I also drove all over Montana and Wyoming and found one of the least populated places I could find, so I could just disappear. I cut my hair, put on some weight, stopped wearing makeup, and dressed plainly. And no one has ever recognized me."

"Do your parents know?"

"Heavens no. I couldn't bear to tell them. And if they found out, I'd just prefer they silently disown me instead of confronting me or asking me about it. They would not take it as well as you have, believe me."

He stood up and turned to face her for the first time. "Terri, I forgive you, not that you did anything against me, but you mentioned forgiveness with respect to this whole thing. So, yes, I forgive you, but I have to be honest - I have some conflicts. You know I lived in LA for a few years also. Part of the fake glitz and glamor that I think of when I remember that place, is the porn industry. In my mind, they are one and the same. I have no problem with anyone who has done it, honestly I don't, but I do believe that some of them immersed themselves into that lifestyle by choice and only left it when they had to because they weren't the fresh face anymore. I have to be able to separate my thoughts of you from my thoughts of that place. Right now.... I can't. Right now, a part of me wonders, are there dark, quiet moments in your life when you miss it – when you crave the action, the adrenaline?"

"Mel, no, that's…"

"Please let me finish. In my life, I have been constantly amazed and bewildered by peoples' various phobias, proclivities and addictions. I've seen addicted gamblers who don't drink. Alcoholics who don't gamble. Fighters afraid to drive fast. And race car drivers afraid to fight. These things that make us human, we usually keep close to us where others can't see. You've revealed something to me tonight so completely out of character for you. Something I could have never guessed. I appreciate the honesty and the courage, I truly do. I know you wouldn't have done it unless you were serious about me, but now you have to give me time to reconcile this with who I thought you were. And when I am finally able to, I will have something for you to reconcile about me. "

"What? What is it Mel? Why not now? Let's get this all out in the air, Mel. Why not now?"

"Because among all those phobias, proclivities and addictions, I also have them. And I can only handle one part of this…equation… at a time."

"You won't leave will you?"

"No, of course not."

"OK," she seemed relieved at that. "We can just…keep talking…"

"No I don't think so." He replied flatly. "I mean, not about this. I have no trouble being around you, Terri. I said I forgive you and I meant it. I'll have no difficulty at our morning coffee and all that, but we can't talk about "us" for a while. I have to process that on my own. I don't know if that is a guy thing, or just a me thing, but it's what I have to do."

She remained stooped over on the couch and he allowed his hand to brush across her hair as he walked past. She reached up to grab his hand, but he was out of reach and she lacked the courage to go after him. He had already indulged her more than she thought he would. She owed him the time and space now to arrive at his own conclusion.

I Ran to Alva

The Hatchet

After a few weeks of gathering materials, acquiring tools and making measurements and calculations, it was finally time to construct the bridge. This particular area where the creek crossed the property had long been on their list

"You be mindful of that ol' fence," Lester admonished Mel above the busy hum of the tractor's engine. The spinning post hole digger that hung off the tractor's tail was within a few inches of rusty old barbwire fencing laying on the ground. Lester was concerned the barbwire might get tangled up in the spinning auger and cause who knows what kind of damage to man or machine.

"I got it," Mel replied impatiently. "Just lower the damn thing, would ya?" His impatience was a hangover of sorts from the ongoing tension he was experiencing with his feelings for Terri and the burden of his guilt, knowing he had yet to come clean about his own past, as she had.

Lester cautiously pushed the tractor's hydraulic lever, lowering the spinning auger to the ground as Mel guided it to the spot for the posthole. It was barely an inch below the surface when it struck an unseen rock, skipped sideways and grabbed the tangled barbwire. In an instant, the wire was a whirling, gnashing monster that slashed and cut everything it touched - . especially Mel. The moment he saw the contact, he tried to step away, but before he could move, the whirling ball of rusty barbwire slashed across his right arm and neck. Lester immediately disengaged the PTO to stop it, but had to dive off the tractor for his own safety, knowing it would take a few seconds for the implement to stop spinning.

Mel's shirt sleeve was shredded and his arm bled profusely. He felt blood flowing down his neck, so he ripped off the remainder of the sleeve and put it against the neck wound to contain the bleeding. After a couple seconds, he removed it to have a look and was stunned at the amount of blood in the fabric. It was a deep, serious cut. He immediately started walking toward the house. "Lester, come with me. I'll need your help."

Lester heard the nervousness in Mel's voice. He couldn't see what was wrong with him, but given the pace at which he was moving, it had to be bad. Lester jogged to catch up with him, and as he got closer, noticed Mel clutching his neck. When he got next to him, he was stunned by the saturation of blood in the makeshift bandage. "Holy shit, Mel!"

"Yeah, I know. I'm sorry I didn't listen to you Lester. I should have moved that fence like you said. I'm sorry."

"Damn boy! We ain't got to worry 'bout that now. We gotta get you to the hospital! Right now! We gon' need Miss Terri to drive. I hope she's here, she was gonna run off to Hulett for that meetin' with them 4-H kids."

"She's not here, I saw her leave. We'll take my truck. You drive."

"We gon' havta get you to Spearfish. They got the only 'mergency room 'round here. It's 40 miles."

"Then you'll have to drive fast."

The two men hastily got into the truck and roared out the driveway in a cloud of dust.

"I'm gonna keep my cell phone handy," Mel said, "in case I start to get light headed, we may need to call for an ambulance and meet them halfway. Do you know how to use one Lester?"

"Oh hell no," he emphatically replied.

Mel could only manage a little snicker at the older man's techno-phobia. "You touch the numbers, 911, just like a regular phone and then hit this red button that says 'send'", he explained as he held the phone up for Lester to see.

"OK, that's simple enough, but don't go doin' anythin' to make me need it. You just lay over there and rest and stop all yer jabberin'."

"I'll be fine Lester," Mel smiled at him, "but let's not take any chances. Get it rollin'. It'll do 85 all day long, so put the pedal down."

He cautiously applied more throttle and the big diesel engine effortlessly pushed the truck faster. When the speedometer read 80 mph, he decided to keep it there and not risk further danger knowing that his reflexes were not what they used to be. He hadn't had his old Dodge over 65 mph in a few years, so this was Indy 500 stuff for him. He marveled at how smooth and composed the big crew cab was at speed, and rather quiet to boot. He'd have really enjoyed himself if not for the circumstances.

To Lester's relief, Mel was remaining conscious and alert. He had to be in great pain, but he didn't moan or carry on in any way. Tough kid, Lester thought, but when they were about five minutes from Spearfish, Mel gazed at Lester with that "far away look" of a man about to pass out. "How far to the hospital?" he asked Lester in a weak voice.

"Just a few miles....you OK?"

"No. I'm gonna black out. Call 911 and tell them we're on our way. Tell them I will need O positive blood. Got it? O Positive...O Positive....." he said as he fell unconscious.

"Oh my GOD!" Lester yelled as he watched Mel slump sideways against the door. With shaking hands, he dialed 911, dropping the truck onto the road shoulder twice as he dialed. When the operator answered, he tried to remain calm, but his voice was quivering. "We on our way to 'mergency at Spearfish! Man's hurt! Bleedin' bad! Passed out! He said his blood type is O positive! We be there in just a couple minutes! I need somebody hep me get 'im out the truck – he's a big dude. Please hep me."

The operator calmed him down by asking routine questions and verifying that Lester knew the proper directions to get to Spearfish General. She assured him that the ER techs were waiting for him to arrive. He was still on the phone with her when he pulled into the hospital driveway. "Thank ye ma'am. I'm here, I gotta go! Thank ye!" But he didn't know how to end the call, so he just set the phone down on the seat and figured he could do it later.

The three ER techs swarmed the truck, one dove inside and two stood by the passenger door to catch Mel when they opened it. The techs asked Lester a rapid succession of questions about Mel's injuries as they laid him on the gurney and whisked him into the hospital. Another tech was waiting in the hallway with a bag of blood. She approached the gurney, attached the bag to the elevated hook, extended the feed line and inserted the needle into his arm without even slowing down. The team hurriedly rolled the gurney into an exam room where a couple doctors were waiting. The automatic doors closed behind them and Lester was left standing alone in the hallway. Suddenly it was just… quiet. He became aware of his hands and knees shaking and wasn't quite sure where to go from here.

"Sir," the young medical assistant called to him in a friendly voice. "Why don't you come with me and help me fill out some information on your son?"

"Oh…..yes miss," Lester stammered, "only he ain't my son, we work together, but he is a… friend. He is a good fr…." And tears rolled down his cheeks as his throat tightened and he found himself unable to speak. She took him gently by the arm and walked him slowly up the hallway to the office. He walked with his head down, his tears dotting a trail on the floor behind him. All the while she said nothing, knowing that he would be inconsolable for a few minutes. She opened the door to the office, led him to a seat by her desk and gestured for him to sit. She offered him some water and he merely nodded. He drank it in small sips for a couple minutes while she began some preliminary work on her computer, knowing he would talk when he was ready.

"Thank you miss, I feel a little better now. Can you check with them docs and see what they think about Mel? How's he doin' and all?"

"Of course I will. Could you tell me his name so I can at least give them something to write on the patient ID tag?

"Yeah, it's Mel, uh, Melvin Hatcher."

"Does he have a middle name?

"Don't rightly know. I suspect he does, but I don't know it. Some friend I am, huh?"

"Sir, stop blaming yourself. I don't know half my friends' middle names or birthdays, its allright."

"Mmmm, hey but I do know his birthday! It's August 1st, we just celebrated it a few weeks ago."

"Great! What year, do you know?"

"Uh, well he said he was 28, so whatever year that is."

"That's fantastic; I probably have all the info I need for a real ID. Thank you so much. Now I will go see the doctors and see how he's doing."

"Thank ye miss."

When she left the room, it occurred to Lester that he ought to reach Terri somehow and let her know what happened. He thought of Mel's cell phone and figured her number might be stored in it. He'd heard these modern phones could store numbers like that and some of them even took pictures and would hook up to that Internet Web thing. He could probably find someone here at the hospital that knew about these things and could help him retrieve Terri's number. He walked outside and moved the truck to an actual parking spot, then picked up Mel's phone and headed back in.

As he entered, the young medical assistant greeted him with a question. "Is there any chance that your friend Melvin is going by his middle name? Is his first name actually Dominic?"

Lester thought for a second. "Yeah, I believe that's right. I believe I remember Miss Terri – she's our boss – saying Mel was not his first name, but I never heard what it was. That could be."

"Good, then I'm certain we have the right person in the records." She walked away, writing something on the papers she had clutched in her elbow.

"How's he doin'?" Lester called to her.

She stopped and walked back to him. "Doctors said his injuries are no longer life threatening," she said softly, "but he lost a lot of blood...a *lot* of blood" she continued with raised eyebrows. "Ten more minutes, and they probably could not have saved him."

"Holy mother of God, are you serious?" Lester was in shock.

"Yes," she affirmed, "but they have him stabilized now. He'll be OK in a couple days, but we'll need to keep him here for observation. And he won't be going back to work for a while."

Lester nodded, took a deep breath and considered what he had thus far failed to fully grasp. Mel had come within 10 minutes of dying. That was a thought. Still, he was gonna be OK now, Lester consoled himself. He had to tell Terri. "Miss, do you reckon you could look at Mel's phone here and maybe find Miss Terri's number in it, so's I can call her?"

"Of course," she said, taking the phone from him. She scrolled through the list of contacts "You said Terri?"

"Yes miss."

"Here it is. Want me to make the call for you?"

"Oh, would you? That'd be dandy. I'm a little rattled right now."

"Of course. And you said Terri is his employer?"

"Yes miss."

She hit Send and listened intently as the phone rang, but was not answered. So she left a voicemail at the prompt; "Hello, this is Amanda, I am the Emergency Room medical assistant at Spearfish General and I am trying to reach Terri with some information about your employee, Dominic Melvin Hatcher. Another employee of yours, Lester, is also here with Mr. Hatcher and said that I should contact you. Please call back this cell phone to speak to Lester or you can reach me at the ER desk. Thank you."

"She didn't answer, huh?"

"No, sorry, but I bet she'll call back on this phone, so here's what you do when it rings." And she gave him a quick lesson in how to answer an incoming call. "Now I have to get back to entering Mr. Hatcher's information at my desk up front, OK? Why don't you walk up there with me so you can be more comfortable in the waiting room?"

"I reckon."

An hour passed before a young doctor walked out to give Lester an update. "We had to do a lot of stitches on your friend, but he was lucky, none of the veins or arteries were badly damaged. A couple days' rest in here, some good meals and he'll be OK, but he will have to take it easy for several days. Lucky, though, you got him here as fast as you did. It was pretty close."

"Allright then, I 'preciate you all takin' care of him. When can I see him?"

"Ohhhh," the young physician hesitated as he thought, "it'll be at least a couple hours before he wakes up and even then, he won't be much for talking, but you're welcome to wait in his room if you like. Visiting hours are over at 9PM, though, unless you are immediate family."

"Oh, no I ain't family, but that's OK I reckon. I'll sit with him and maybe he'll wake up 'fore I have to go."

"Allright, sir." The young doctor escorted Lester down the hall and quietly opened the door to Mel's room. "I'll be back in a half hour or so to check in on him. You can stretch out on the little couch there if you want to and there are vending machines down at the end of the hall if you need a drink or a snack."

"Thank ye doc," Lester said with a sincere smile and a firm handshake. He stepped into Mel's room, thinking he needed to be quiet so as not to disturb him, but such precaution was hardly necessary. He sat down on the couch and stared intently at the bandages that covered Mel's arm and neck. He found it odd that the bandaging gave barely a clue about the extent of the damage. What was that above the bandage on his arm? A tattoo? He hadn't seen that before, Mel always wore sleeves. Looked like an axe or something. It seemed to Lester a peculiar thing for a man to have tattooed on his arm. Then he remembered the sight of Mel's shirt completely saturated with blood and the way it had covered the seat and some of the carpeting in the truck. It was a small miracle, wasn't it, that Mel was alive at all? The thought of the young man being so close to death suddenly hit home to Lester and he began sobbing. He shoved his face hard into the palms of his hands to try and squelch the noise, ever mindful of Mel sleeping nearby. His hands could not contain the flood of tears and they made their way down his forearms and onto his pants. He remained so for a couple minutes, until he was finally able to compose himself and sit upright. Then he noticed the little box of tissues by the sink and pulled several to wipe his face.

Just then Mel's phone began playing a song. It startled and bewildered Lester, and he wondered if he had accidentally pushed a button to make it play. How would he turn it off? It was kind of funny, though, he was pretty certain he'd heard the song before and when he looked at the display, it was flashing "Terri". Suddenly Lester understood the ringtone and almost laughed out loud. He knew that Mel and Terri sometimes had words and Mel must have put this song on his phone after one of those times. He answered the call per the instructions Amanda had given him.

"Lester Lester…what the hell is going on?!?!?! Are you guys at the hospital?!?!?!" Terri began. There was real concern in her voice and she was not predisposed to swearing. He gave her the play-by-play of what had happened and it sounded to him like she was crying, though she denied it when he asked her. "I'm coming right away; I'll be there in an hour."

"Oh now Miss Terri, you don't need to go to all that fuss. Mel is asleep and besides it'll be almost nine by the time you get here and they'll just make us leave anyway. Only family gets to stay past nine."

"Then I will tell them I'm his sister," she replied defiantly. "I'll see you in an hour." The phone went silent and Lester stared at it for a moment before he figured out that he didn't actually have to do anything to "hang up."

He managed to relax a bit on the little couch, comforted in the knowledge that Terri was coming and he wouldn't be alone with an injured Mel. He dozed off and while he slept, the doctor came in, checked Mel's vitals, adjusted his IV line, made some entries on his chart and left without a sound.

174

"Lester....Lester....." Terri was whispering to him quietly and tapping his shoulder. He came to rather abruptly and sat up.

"Oh Miss Terri, I am so glad you're here. It was an awful thing, just awful." She sat next to him and put her arm around his shoulder as he again recounted what happened, but in more detail this time.

"And he could have died?" she asked again in disbelief.

"Yes ma'am, docs said 10 more minutes like that and he'd a been a goner. And you know what? He musta known. He told me how fast to drive. He told me how to call 911 right before he passed out. He even told me his blood type so's I could tell them E.R. people in advance. He musta known it was bad, but he didn't say nuthin'. He was more calm than me. Damn, such a thing…"

Terri really couldn't say much and she could sense Lester was on the verge of breaking into tears, so she just sat quietly with her arm around him and said nothing. After a few minutes, a nurse walked in and announced that it was 9PM and only immediate family was allowed to stay. She was very courteous and kind about it, but rules were rules and Terri understood that.

"OK," Lester said as he stood. Then he turned to Terri. "Sure am glad you was able to rush down here from Billings. You take good care of your *brother*. If you don't mind, I'll take his phone so's you can reach me and I'll see you in the mornin'."

"Ahhh, yeah, OK…."Terri stammered as she took a second to recall her claim as Mel's sister and catch up to what Lester was saying. "Are you going back to Alva now?"

"Naaa, I have an old friend lives a ways outta town here. I'll just go over and sleep on his couch tonight, he won't mind."

"You're his sister?" the nurse inquired.

"Yesss," Terri responded unconvincingly.

"Ummmm, OK, well, in that case…….. you can stay…." She looked repeatedly at Terri and Lester, doubting the story…."This couch folds out to a small bed if you decide to sleep here and I will get you some sheets and a pillow and what-not."

"That would be great, thank you so much."

"Allrighty Miss…….Theresa", Lester was careful to use her real first name, as he was certain "Terri" was written somewhere on one of those documents as Mel's employer. "I'll be a goin' now. See you in the mornin'…'bout maybe ten or so."

"OK Lester, see you then. And Lester…."she paused. "You did really great. You were great. You saved his life. You really did. Thank you."

Lester couldn't even respond with words, so he merely nodded and shrugged awkwardly before leaving the room.

The nurse got `Theresa` situated with all the linens she'd need and then left her with Mel. She sat quietly on the couch for a while, but then curiosity got the best of her and she stood to take a closer look at Mel's bandaging. The one on the neck was not very big at all, but given its location, she understood how it could have easily been fatal. She stared at it for quite some time and then turned her attention to his arm. Those bandages covered a lot more area, but it didn't look like any huge gaps of flesh were missing beneath them, so she reasoned as how they probably weren't too serious compared to the neck. And even though he had held her a couple times, she had never seen him sleeveless before, so she was rather surprised at the size and muscular definition of his arms and shoulders. What was written under that tattoo? She peered closely at the tiny script..."The Hatchet". So the little tattoo was not an axe, but a hatchet. She figured it was a play on his last name, probably given to him by his old buddies or....an old flame. Hmmmm. If it was the latter, it would explain why he kept it covered up.

She sat down and busied herself with sending a few texts to people who would want to know where she was and what she was up to. She quietly pulled out the hide-a-bed and worked everything onto the thin mattress that was certain to be uncomfortable. The prospect of sleeping in less than desirable conditions really didn't bother her much, as she usually just did the best with whatever was on hand. It did occur to her, however, that she would not be able to sleep in her favorite loose fitting sweats. That was a bummer.

Her phone hummed quietly over the next several minutes as she received and answered texts from various friends and associates. She ignored the question from her uncle, though, "So will *this* finally make you push him for an answer?" That was too big a question for her to handle right now. She switched off the phone and decided to get some sleep.

She removed her shoes, socks and the bulky sweatshirt, but then hesitated at removing her jeans. She looked carefully at Mel for any sign of consciousness, but then removed them and slid quickly beneath the sheet and blanket. She deliberately laid on her right side, as she could see his face from that angle and would likely awaken more quickly if anything happened. His utter lack of movement was a little worrisome. She thought he should twitch or move his head or something, but all the instruments hooked up to him appeared to show good numbers, lines and dots, so she took some comfort in that. About 5 minutes of staring at him, wondering "what if", was a sobering thought process.

He was a good man, it seemed. He barely drank, didn't smoke anything, never swore, had an even temper, worked hard, was kinda smart and strong as a bull. And he sure was good looking, as her few friends frequently pointed out. It was interesting, though, why he came to Alva. More interesting, she thought, was what she didn't know. The guy left California for a $10.00 an hour job as a ranch hand and showed up in a $50,000 truck pulling a $30,000 trailer that was carrying a motorcycle and a big ATV, both worth $10,000 apiece. He had no debts, no legal troubles, nobody looking for him, clean as a whistle. She understood and believed his story about the abuse he suffered at the hands of sports agents and trainers, and that was why he left everything. She understood about running out of LA. She understood about some of the people in LA. She had been afraid to ask him too many questions, truth be told, because maybe she didn't want him to get resentful over the hurdle he was trying to cross with her own background.

It was funny, though, that she had never thought until that moment to even ask him what sport he had been involved in. That should be an innocent enough question, shouldn't it? The more she thought of it, the more she reasoned that "the Hatchet" was probably a nickname his teammates gave him. And why, she wondered, didn't he just move to some other city and resume his sports career? Why just pitch everything, everything he knew and lived for to take up a laborer's wage more than a thousand miles away? That was indeed a deep question and a trifle … troubling. She needed to know more, but soon she drifted off to sleep and slept through the two bed checks the nurse made during the night.

She awoke to find Mel engaged in a quiet conversation with the attending physician. She laid still and observed them quietly, not wanting to disturb them, but was also being a little sneaky. She reasoned as how Mel might be willing to have a more candid conversation with the doc if he believed she was still asleep. If so, she'd learn more about his condition. Their chat was not particularly revealing, except for the part where the doc coached Mel into not saying anything about Terri being his employer. He told Mel that the nurses here were sticklers about such things and would throw her out if they learned she was indeed not family. Then he turned to leave and Terri snapped her eyes shut.

After a few seconds, Mel began calling to her.

"Terri…….hey Terri….psssst….Terri,"

She opened her eyes and pretended to be confused for a moment. "What? Oh….you're awake."

"Yeah…… when did you get here?"

"Last night, about nine I think. Oh, my name is Theresa, and I'm your sister."

He looked back at her with the most curious stare. "I am awake, right?"

She chuckled lightly, "Yes. That's the story I had to give the charge nurse, or else they'd have made me leave last night."

"Oh, yeah, OK, sure, I get it. Theresa. Close enough."

"That's my real name."

"For real? Why didn't I know that?"

"You didn't ask."

"Yeah…..fair enough….hey where is Lester? Man, I really owe him big time. Poor guy, I really scared him. Is he OK? I sure want to thank him. I knew when I blacked out that it was all up to him, but I knew he'd get me here."

"He wasn't the only one who you scared." Her eyes bored in on him and she didn't look away, as she always had before. He could only stare back into those eyes, they had him and he was the one who wanted to look away this time, but he couldn't. Was she the one now who was seeing the conflict within him? Had the roles really reversed? For sure they had, only he was the one now who had something to reveal and something to fear. The very real trauma that put him in this bed was giving him perspective and giving it fast. What did her past matter? He…..loved her. He did. And all the while he pondered these things, her eyes bored into his and he knew, somehow he knew, that she read every thought he'd just had.

"I'm sorry, Terri. I violated one of the few laws of heavy machinery – never operate when distracted."

"Why were you distracted?"

"You. Us."

"There's us?"

"There might be. Only that decision is not going to be up to me." He looked awkwardly down at the bed and his surroundings. He became aware that his gown had crept up his arm, revealing the tattoo. He tried to casually pull it down to cover it without her noticing, but he saw her eyes divert to it and knew he'd failed. "You made a revelation. You made it because you cared enough about me to be honest. Sure it was a pretty big deal, but…"

"Yes?"

"It's pretty tame compared to what I need to tell you. You're a vestial virgin compared to me. And I feel pretty silly now, having balked and hesitated these past couple weeks."

"Does it have anything to do with that tattoo?"

"Yes."

"Perhaps the best way to tell you is simply the way you showed me. Get on the internet and…"

"No. No Mel. I won't do it. I don't even want to hear it. I don't want to know. What I revealed to you, wasn't that damage enough? We're good people who made mistakes, Mel. What good will it do now to keep dragging all our skeletons out of

181

the closets? Just let it stop. Whatever it is, I want to be with you. Just let it go. It isn't that bad."

He wanted to believe her, to embrace her sentiments, but he could see a day, maybe 6 months, maybe 6 years from now, when the information would hit her full in the face and he'd look into those deep amazing eyes and all they would say back to him is "you monster." But he was too tired to argue, the loss of blood was sapping his strength and his focus. He lay back down and closed his eyes, but he held out his hand and was happy to feel her take it right before he fell asleep.

He grew stronger over the next couple days and was released to Lester and Terri's care. Doug, Molly and Sarah were there to see him released. Per hospital protocol, the nurses had to roll him out to his truck in a wheelchair which he vehemently protested, and his protests were summarily ignored.

"Be quiet and enjoy the ride," Terri said with a smile. This is the last time anyone's gonna be moving your big butt around."

Doug laughed robustly at the way Terri spoke so comfortably to him. Didn't matter that neither of them had formally acknowledged it, Terri was speaking to "her" man. Mel took note of Doug's laughter and inquired, "Does Molly speak to you like that?"

"All the time," he laughed.

Terri said nothing, but she was pleased that Mel had looked at the couple who'd been married 15 years and was maybe seeing himself in Doug's place. For sure, Doug and Molly were one of the happiest couples she'd ever known and their daughter Sarah was a joy to be around. It'd be cool to have a kid like Sarah…

"What? Passenger side?" Mel protested. "I wanna drive – it's my truck."

"Not today, cowboy," said Terri, again asserting her authority. "Climb on up there and be quiet."

Lester found the whole thing very amusing and was giggling as he climbed into the rear passenger side door. After a bunch of "thank you's" and "blessings", the big truck finally rolled out the drive and headed for home, complete with an escort. It was a cool, sunny autumn day and the wind blowing into the open window was exactly what Mel needed after 3 days of artificial light and sterilized everything. He needed sun, wind, dirt and motion. He also needed and craved physical activity, but he would wait for that per the doctor's orders.

When Terri wheeled the big Ford into the driveway, Mel off-handedly said "Good to be home." It pleased her, as she didn't know he thought of it that way, but the happiness surged up in her to the point that she had trouble fighting back tears. Would he want to make it his home? Things were improving between them, but it was by no means a done deal. She thought of how funny it was, in all the time they'd known each other and for all the talks they'd had about so many deep subjects and such personal topics; they'd only ever kissed once. That night at the fair in the Tilt-o-Whirl, but a kiss like that can carry people for a mighty long way.

I Ran to Alva

One Trip Around the Sun

Terri was glad to see the lights of home after such a long drive back from Billings. Getting a late start hadn't helped matters, but it was always so hard to say goodbye to her uncle. She had grown so close to him over the past two years and his failing health made her a bit anxious. She was not ready to let go of him yet, she was still not her own person, not yet healed, as it were. And the situation with Mel wasn't helping her feel secure. She thought he was working through the shock of her background and he said that he was making progress, but then the accident happened with the posthole digger. He had said he was fine with whatever her past had been, but then he seemed fixated on revealing something from his own past that she told him repeatedly she didn't want or need to know. But he couldn't get past it; he kept insisting that she needed to know.

As she rolled up the driveway, it seemed strange that the awning lights were still on outside Mel's trailer and she wondered if he was up late working on something. She pulled nearer the house and looked for signs of activity by the trailer but saw none. As she exited the little Toyota, curiosity got the better of her and she walked a little closer. That's when she noticed him laying on the artificial turf rug just outside the trailer. She rushed to him to assess his injuries, hopeful that he wasn't too badly hurt. She wondered if it was somehow related to the barb wire injury and was scared that it might be. When she reached his side, she gently nudged him to see if he was anywhere near conscious. She was startled and a little bewildered by what she found.

185

He reeked of alcohol and there was an empty, overturned glass lying near his outstretched right hand. She guessed whiskey. She thought in a moment of annoyance about just leaving him there to suffer his own consequences, but then she reconsidered, because something must be wrong. This did not fit. Mel was not a power drinker. He was sometimes seen with a stout in his hand after dinner, but seldom did she see him with a second one. So many times she'd overheard Lester giving him a hard time about his lack of drinking prowess and she'd laugh as the older man would tease him about being such a candy ass whose drinking philosophy was "one and done." Why would Mel do this to himself? She wondered. She nudged at his shoulder to see if there was any response. He smiled and mumbled a couple incoherent words, so she nudged him again.

"What do you want?" he mumbled.

"Mel… you should get up and go inside. You passed out."

"Bug fu**ing deal," he spoke with a little more clarity.

Terri was stunned at his f-bomb, as he seldom used any profanity. "C'mon Mel, you should go inside," she persisted. "You'll catch a cold or something. C'mon, get up and go inside."

"You should just………shtay away….frommmmmmm me," he murmured while still laying on the ground in his alcoholic daze. "Because…because…I'm a killer….you see….and it's only been a year. Only a year. Has it only been a year? Since I killed him? Is that all?" He looked at Terri with half-closed eyes, expecting an answer to his question.

"I don't know Mel,"she replied uncertainly, "who are we talking about?"

"Phillip of course! What kind of dumb-ass question is that?" He practically yelled, though it seemed as though his ire was not meant for her.

"Who is Phillip? Who are you talking about Mel? You didn't kill anyone."

"Oh! Oh but I did! C'monnnnn...c'mon......Terri...come with me," he slurred as he struggled to rise to his feet. "Come with me and I will show you the evidence. I'll show you... how I killed my best friend... on pay per view. No bullshit," he asserted. "It's all fu**ing true, every word of it. I'm a vicious and vindictive killer," he continued to rave amid drunken, animated gestures with his hands. "Come along...Terri...and I will show you."

It was obvious to her that he was sincere in this proclamation of having killed someone, but exactly *what* he was sincere about, she could not fathom. This man was not a straight up killer, she was utterly certain of that. Still, he was adamant, so she indulged his offer, if only to put her curiosity to rest. "Allright Mel, you show me. Can you walk OK?"

"Well...." He stammered, "That is the...what is it? The sixty four thousand dollar question, I guess," he replied as he rose upon shaky legs, laughing. "Do you know what that phrase means, 'cuz I don't, but my parents said it all the time, so I just repeat it. How 'bout you, boss?"

"It's from an old tv game show," she replied. Her tone reflected more of annoyance at his inebriated state than

187

indulgence. She got him into the trailer and figured she'd just point him toward his bed to sleep it off, and maybe he could tell her tomorrow about whom he killed and why.

But when he got near the laptop, he pointed to it, "There you go Miss Terri, I mean….boss…." he stammered as he wobbled on unsteady legs. "You just touch any old key and watch the video. It's so charming…. what they can do….. on video these days. Somebody……. took the time and trouble to document…. every word I said….. and then made this really nice video with all my nasty remarks and then….. and then….. showed in slow motion how I killed my best friend."

At this point, Terri was a little nervous. Clearly Mel was not just embellishing a story or exaggerating a conflict. She was about to see something she could not unsee and if Mel was right, might change everything. She braced herself, touched the finger pad on the laptop and the video segment was there, ready to hit replay. So she did.

It started showing footage from a….what did they call it? A cage fight. That was it. The commentators were talking about how a guy named Phillip Washington was unexpectedly pummeling the favored contender, Dom Hatcher, "The Hatchet" as they called him. It was Mel, and she could hardly draw a breath. He had been a cage fighter? The last piece of that footage showed him being knocked unconscious by a scary looking kick to the head. The referee waved it over, the bell rang and the video changed. It was Mel, sporting a goatee, talking to an interviewer. He was discussing that fight and the knockout and how he was gonna makes Phillip pay. There was a rematch scheduled and he was gonna beat Phillip into submission. "I'll kill that bastard," he said flatly, looking straight in to the camera. Terri was stunned, she felt her face get flush and hot and felt a wave of denial washing over her. There was no way that steely-eyed monster on the video was Mel. It just couldn't be. She turned to look at him.

He was still rocking and shifting on his feet, unsteady as any drunk, but he slurred, "Go on…go on…..keeeeeeeeep watching. It just gets better."

The video then showed the introductions to their fight rematch. The commentators were clearly enjoying the storyline, how these two men had started together as rookies, become very good friends and never had to fight each other because they were in different weight classes. Then Phillip Washington moved up in weight to Dominic Hatcher's class and it put them on a collision course. As Terri had already seen, Phillip won the first fight, but in the interview excerpts on the video, it was clear that The Hatchet …Mel… was in a rage and bent on revenge. He declared that his friendship with Phillip was history and he was going to destroy him. Then the video moved forward to the 2nd round of the fight. It showed Phillip's face already bloodied, but he was still steady on his feet and looking plenty strong. The menacing look on Mel's face….what was that, Terri wondered? He looked like an animal, stalking something he intended to kill, though not just yet. There were a couple exchanges of fists, followed by separations, both of which Mel had scored points and hurt Phillip some more. Then…

Phillip launched a high arcing kick, known as a roundhouse, which Mel adroitly ducked. As Phillip continued spinning from the momentum of the kick, Mel charged. He struck him twice in the abdomen with vicious blows, the second of which sent

Phillip against the perimeter fencing of the cage. He went into it with his back and the tensile springiness of the fencing propelled him forward in Mel's direction. Mel launched a full-on uppercut punch that he timed perfectly to catch Phillip's chin. His powerful arm and hand were going in exactly the opposite direction of Phillip's head and were at the strongest point of their extension when the fist and chin impacted. Phillips was already unconscious when he fell to the floor and, once on the floor, there was no sign of movement. Or life. Basal stem cell trauma, the doctors called it. The blow had struck so firmly that the skull literally ripped itself apart from the nerve bundle at the top of the spinal cord, similar to what happened to Dale Earnhardt in the Daytona 500. The greatest shock for Terri was Mel's behavior. He stood just a few feet away from Phillip's lifeless body, taunting, "I told you I'd fu**ing kill you, you maggot! I told you!!"

Then the video ended with a still picture of Mel's face and the word "Killer" in bright red letters across the screen. After a couple seconds, the letters began pulsating and Terri could watch no more. She slammed down the laptop screen and stared at the floor, her heart racing and her mind screaming "NO!"

"Charming, eh?" Mel mumbled. "There's the high point of my life right there, Miss....Terri....I mean, boss....right there on that video. That's what the whole sporting world knows me for. Woo hooo! I'm a vicious fu**ing killer."

She didn't know what to say to him. She stood on shaky legs and tried to gather her thoughts, but it was certainly coming together for her. His physique, his expensive truck and trailer rig, why he was just so willing to abandon his life and run. Just run. Yet she knew about running, and she obviously knew that not everything on video is as it seems. This was difficult, though. The man on the video seemed genuinely interested in being who he was, he seemed to relish the fact that he had beaten a man into unconsciousness and displayed no remorse when officials failed to revive him.

"Mel," she said softly,"I want you to sleep this off and we will talk tomorrow. If you want to. All I can tell you is the man I've gotten to know is not that man I saw on the screen. That is not you."

"Ohhhhh, bosssssssssssssss," he slurred, smiling and waving his hand dismissively, "It's all right there on video. There's my face, there's what I did, that's who I am," he finished, looking up at the ceiling. And tears streamed down his cheeks. "Phillip had been my best friend… and I got angry because he moved up into…. My…… weight class. And then….. he beat me in our first match. I hated him. And I killed him. I killed him," and he had to stop talking because he was being choked by the tears.

"Mel. Mel, listen to me. Things happen that spin out of control. People do things or say things that really aren't what they are about. People get desperate, or angry, or whatever, and behave in ways that are not normal for them. You know I know that Mel." She wondered if any of this was getting through, given his state.

"That'sssss niccccccccce, Miss Terri," he responded with some disdain in his voice. "I appreciate you trying to make me feel better, but all you did was take your clothes off and do what everyone does naturally. But…heyyyyyy, I appreciate your sentiments."

"Go to sleep now Mel. Go sleep this off. I won't have Lester wake you until noon. We'll talk more tomorrow." And her voice had a little more authority to it, so Mel cooperated.

"Allllllllllrighty boss, I'll hit the hay. Just following orders, ma'am," as he gave her a mock salute and turned toward his bedroom. She watched him amble up the narrow hallway and then turned to leave when she saw he made it to his room, though barely.

She wondered if he would remember the conversation tomorrow. She wondered if he would remember anything tomorrow. She wondered if she would see him tomorrow. She knew just enough about drinking that light drinkers who get hammered, pay a severe price the next day. She decided to just tell Lester to leave him alone for the day and she wondered how she'd ever be able to console him or to convince him in any meaningful way that she could truly empathize. Still, that wasn't really the core of the problem was it? The real problem was he couldn't forgive himself. So she began to understand a little of his thought process. If he could not forgive himself, then how could anyone else for give him? That was the hot mess confronting him, and her.

I Ran to Alva

Redeeming the Time

The weeks that followed Mel's accident and the drunken revelation of his violent past put a chill on the Team worse than the changing of Wyoming from fall to winter. Through Lester's insistence, they still met almost every morning for their coffee planning session, but it had been moved from Mel's trailer to Terri's house. The first couple meetings in her house were necessitated by Mel's trailer having experienced frozen water pipes during an especially nasty chill. No water, no coffee, but then Terri requested they continue to have them in the house. Mel didn't object. He hardly said a word anymore, positive or negative. Lester figured that Terri's desire to move the meetings to her house was a way of not having to go into Mel's trailer. He knew pretty much everything, inasmuch as there had been a budding romance and it looked like things were about to hit their stride. Then the wheels fell off the wagon. Day after day, there was only work. There was no camaraderie, no banter, no teasing, no pizza nights, nothing. To Lester, it was such a waste. They were such a natural fit, why couldn't they push past whatever kept them apart?

One early December morning, Mel's phone rang. It was Doug.

"How've you been Mel? Recovered by now I hope?"

Mel was happy to hear his voice. "Sure have. All healed up, strong as an ox. I took it easy for a couple weeks, but then eased back into it. Now it's like it never happened."

"I'm so glad to hear that, truly. How's Terri? I haven't seen her much because Molly has been taking Sarah to the 4-H meetings since my evenings are busier now."

"Terri's, uhhh, fine. Why did your evenings get busy?"

"Oh, I was made principal at the high school after Bradley Williams retired. So now I am faced with occasional evening meetings. PTA, Booster clubs, that sort of thing."

"Ah, well, congratulations on the promotion. I didn't know you were a teacher, or administrator or whatever."

"Yes, I guess we never talked much about our occupations, but you did mention one thing about your background, and that is why I am calling."

"Oh?"

You may remember you told me of your high school and junior college wrestling career and that you had continued to wrestle in various amateur leagues after you left school."

"Sure, I remember."

"Well, I also remember Terri teasing you about having workout equipment in your trailer and all the running and bike riding you do. "

Mel began to sense this was going somewhere, but couldn't connect the dots. "So, are you about to ask something related to all that?"

"Yes Mel," Doug answered with a chuckle. "Our assistant wrestling coach was badly injured in a car crash last week and we need someone to step in. I am asking if you're interested."

"Well......," he stammered, "I mean, I guess so, yeah, but I need to know more. Like the schedule and all. It can't interfere with my work here."

"Of course. Well, basically, practice is every school day from 4-6pm. There are matches two nights a week, Tuesday and Thursday, some are here and some are away. And there will be three tournaments during the course of the season that will be done on Saturdays. Oh, and you'll get a whopping $1500 pay for the entire season."

"Hmmm, that schedule might work. Let me talk to Terri about it, though. Can I call you tomorrow?"

"Of course. I'm delighted that you would even consider it. I think you're a good guy, Mel, and I think if you can relate to someone as difficult as Dylan Turner, then I you can certainly get along with these young boys. Oh, but I do have to ask…have you ever been arrested, or convicted of a crime?"

"No, never," he replied. But maybe I ought to have been, he thought.

"Great. That should be really all I need to know. I look forward to hearing from you, no matter what your answer is. Let's stay in touch, and please tell Terri I said hello."

"Sure enough Doug, it was great to hear from you. Bye"

Terri gave no resistance to Mel's interest in the coaching position; she even thought it would do him good to have something additional to occupy his time. She knew he would maintain his work duties around the time demands of the new position, so she gave it her wholehearted blessing. Lester thought it was kind of cool, too, though he acknowledged he'd have to be prepared to carry on more phone discussions with Mel to handle things that cropped up when he wasn't there.

So Mel made the acceptance phone call to Doug, and the next day went over to the high school to sign a few papers and meet Zack Taylor, the head coach. Zack was only about 5 years older than Mel, had been Montana State Champion two years and then got a full ride to wrestling mecca Iowa University. At Iowa, he managed to make it to the Nationals two years but came up a bit short of winning the championships. He used his education at Iowa to full effect, setting himself up to be Physics teacher and wrestling coach. The Physics teacher status was what impressed Mel the most. Wrestling he understood and could speak the lingo, but rotational kinematics and moments of inertia? That was some high minded dialog.

The team practice started the next day. At the beginning, Coach Zack introduced Coach Mel to the team and explained that Coach Mel would be focusing on helping them with their drills and conditioning, while he would be focused on teaching them new techniques and strategy. One kid in particular on the team, was happy to see Coach Mel. Bobby Grayling, wrestling the heavyweight class. Coach Zack was awesome, but was only about 5'6" and 145 pounds. Bobby was 6'4" and 260, though he could have stood to drop 20-30 pounds. Doing drills with Coach Zack was almost impossible, and none of the other boys

196

on the team were nearly big enough or strong enough to challenge him and push him. Bobby had high hopes for his senior season and his new assistant coach looked like a man who could help that happen.

Mel was a natural at coaching young boys. He still had vivid memories of being a boy that age and remembered how easy it was to get rattled when things went wrong. He discovered there was a prevailing mentality among the boys that wrestling was really just a fight without punches or kicks. He believed if he could correct that mindset, that there were a few of the boys who might really shine. After reading a couple books by famous wrestling coaches, he was able to boil it down to a level that the boys could understand.

"Wrestling," he said to them as a group, "is basically a very physical chess match. It is moves and counter moves, and you have to be able to match the other guy's strength and stamina. I can help you with the physical conditioning. I can get you there if you're willing to do the work. Coach Zack can teach you the moves, but you are the only one who can teach yourself to be cool under pressure, to analyze the situation when your opponent is about to stick your shoulders to the mat. If you want to succeed, you have to put these all together: Moves, strategy, strength, stamina. You have to have it in your head that you will work on all these things at the same time."

Coach Zack stood nodding his approval as Mel gave the lesson. He had known all these things in his years, but had never boiled them down so concisely in his own mind. He was optimistic that Mel had found a short, easily understood mantra of sorts that the boys could grasp. And grasp they did. Mel and Zack instilled in them the notion of being a team, instead of a collection of separate wrestlers. They encouraged the 2nd and 3rd tier wrestlers to push the 1st tiers guys just as hard as they could. "If we're going to be a team," Zack admonished, "it is up to each one of us to make everyone better. You're not doing the 1st tier guy any favors by going easy on him. You wrestle him each time as though you have something to prove."

The heavyweight, Bobby Grayling, improved more than all the rest. With a big strong guy like Mel to wrestle against, his technique and stamina improved exponentially over the previous year. He started the season with a loss, but then won 5 straight matches including a victory over the previous year's conference champion. He had also dropped 15 pounds and was getting faster and more agile. His self-esteem was definitely on the rise and Mel essentially dared him to think about the possibility of competing in the state tournament at the end of the season. At first Bobby said, "That's just stupid, man" but he had stopped saying it and had begun asking questions about advanced wrestling techniques.

The winter moved along through the holidays and into the new year. Mel stayed busy with his duties at the ranch and as Assistant Wrestling Coach. It was a good life, except for the persistent tension between him and Terri. It had gone on for so long now that he had lost focus on what he needed to reconcile within himself. Terri also stayed busy and was actually going to turn a profit through each of the winter months, with the spring and summer looking to be half again better than the previous year. And she loved her girls in the 4-H troop. She often had them over to her house when they needed to congregate and work on something as a group. Nothing like a houseful of giggling girls who talked incessantly about boys, horses and clothes. This part of her life really was charmed. She hoped against hope that one day she'd have a daughter who could experience all the fun and friendship these girls knew. That would require a partner, though, someone to complete the circle. If it wasn't Mel, then it would never be anyone. She made that decision a long time ago and was at peace with it. She only hoped that one day he could find the peace within to forgive himself. She knew he'd have to forgive himself to be able to let go of all the baggage and as long as the baggage was there, he couldn't make room for her.

When school resumed session in the new year, Mel noticed a change in Bobby Grayling's disposition. He'd become withdrawn and quiet. He lost his first two matches, obviously wrestling with not a hint of fire in his belly.

"What do you suppose is going on with Bobby?" Mel asked Zack

"Same thing as last year. His dad died two years ago on New Year's Day."

"Damn, I didn't know. That's sad."

"Yeah, poor kid blames himself."

"Why?"

"His dad told him not to take the snowmobile out, but he did. He snuck out on it for a joy ride and then it broke down. So he called dad to come get him. Dad piled up the truck when he missed a curve and died in the crash. Sheriff Peterson blamed it on excessive speed. He had a temper, so I heard, he was probably pissed off and driving too fast, but the kid blames himself."

Mel's heart sunk when he heard this. To be that young, losing his father, blaming himself. A burden no boy ought to bear. He understood the weight of carrying around guilt for hurting a loved one, but at least people would agree in his own case that he was to blame. Sounded like Bobby would still have a father if the man had simply driven slower, but try telling him that. Still, a thought occurred to Mel. A risky thought, but probably worth it. Someone had to figuratively "hit" this kid to get him back onto the right track in life. Maybe it would work, maybe it wouldn't, but not trying wasn't an option.

That evening, he approached Terri and discussed the situation with her about Bobby and told her what he planned to do. She was generally in favor, but pointed out the risks that he already considered, plus a couple others he hadn't. She wished him well and thought it was sweet of him to take such a personal interest in the boy.

"When are you going to talk to him?" she asked.

"No time like the present. I looked up his address on the team roster. I'm gonna head over there now. I just wanted to talk to you first to see if you had any pointers. Thanks for the help."

She smiled and then reached out and grabbed his hand. He held it for a moment and felt things melting away as he stared into her eyes. Things always seemed to feel right when he was looking there. He kissed her on the cheek and said he'd be back soon.

"Oh, I almost forgot." He stopped. "Could you look up the non-emergency dispatch number for Sheriff Peterson's office? I need to talk to him."

Terri seemed puzzled but she popped open the laptop and looked up the number. Mel loaded it into his phone and then hit "send" as he walked out the door. The dispatcher answered as he was climbing into the truck. He told her his name and requested to talk to the sheriff regarding the two year old accident and she put him on hold to see if Peterson was available. A few seconds went by and then a click:

"Dominic Melvin Hatcher... how may I be of service to you this evening...?"

Bobby's house was a quarter-mile off the paved road and Mel wondered if he had to walk out every day to catch the bus during the winter mornings. Probably did, but he knew these country kids were tough, so it probably wasn't that big of a deal. Two huskies circled and barked at the truck as he came to a stop next to the small house. He thought about getting out, but wasn't sure how aggressive the pair might be. The porch light came on and he saw Bobby step outside and call to the dogs, so Mel stepped out of the truck and waved to him.

"Coach Mel?" he was very surprised. His mom came to the door and stood behind him. She recognized the name when she heard Bobby call it. Both were pretty stunned to see the wrestling coach in their driveway.

"Yeah, Bobby, hey I wanted to talk to you about something if it's allright."

"Sure, come on in."

Mel walked up the porch, greeted his mom and apologized for showing up unannounced, but he said he had something to talk about and he felt it was urgent. She invited him in and they all sat down at the little dining room table. Judging by the pictures displayed on the wall, Mel saw that Bobby's parents had gotten married very young, would have been barely over twenty when they gave birth to him. It also appeared that he had a younger sister, and then he became aware of a young girl's voice chatting down the hall, probably on the phone.

"Bobby, I'll come to the point. I noticed after the holidays that your wrestling and your focus has been off."

"Yeah, I'm sorry coach, I'll work harder…"

"No, son, let me finish." He surprised himself using that word. It was the first time he had ever called anyone that. He hoped neither the boy nor the mom would take offense and was prepared to apologize, but neither batted an eye. He remembered that rural people often spoke that way to the younger generation, so to them it was no big deal. "When Coach Zack and I were talking about how your wrestling had dropped off, he explained to me about the significance of New Year's Day."

"Ohhh…." And Bobby looked at the floor. His mom reached across to hold his hand. Mel saw a tear streak down the boy's cheek as he began to sniffle.

Mel pulled his wallet out of his back pocket and opened it. He pulled out a folded up newspaper clipping and placed it on the table without opening it. Then he continued.

"I know the burden of feeling like you were responsible for someone's death, Bobby. I also carry it with me."

"Your dad?"

"No, my best friend. Listen, I need to tell you something. I spoke to Sheriff Peterson about your dad's accident."

"You did?"

"Yeah… I have to ask you something…. When you called your dad to come pick you up because the snowmobile had broken down, did you tell him you were hurt or in any danger?"

"No sir, not at all. In fact, I was sitting in old man Ferguson's house. I used his phone. He even fed me lunch. I was fine."

"So you gave your dad no reason to believe you needed him right away, that he needed to hurry?"

"No, but he was pissed…sorry mom… he was angry that I took the snowmobile out. And he always drove fast when he was mad."

Mel could see the light start to go on in Bobby's eyes. "OK, so you took the snowmobile without permission, but when you made the call, you told him you were unharmed and safe. Let me say this with utmost respect to your dad, Bobby. He chose to drive fast. For whatever reason, he decided. He could have driven slower and would probably have made that turn. I know it doesn't hurt any less that he's gone, but the point is, it was his decision that truly led to his death. Not you taking the snowmobile." And he unfolded the newspaper clipping.

"I know the difference between being responsible for someone's death, and not. This man here in the news story, Phillip, was my best friend. We were cage fighters in LA, trained together and everything. Only he fought in a lower weight division than I did so we never fought each other. He eventually moved up to my weight class and I didn't like it. Mine was the premier weight class and I was doing well, I was winning fights and moving up. I was getting press coverage and making money. He wanted to be a part of that, too, and I shouldn't have blamed him. We eventually fought and he beat me. Knocked me out actually. I went nuts. For our re-match I trained like an animal, I talked like an animal and lived like an animal. I denounced him as my friend, both to his face and to the media. All the sports reporters just ate it up, everyone was talking about it. In the rematch, I fought without honor and fought only to hurt him, which I did." And he unfolded another piece of paper which made Bobby and his mom's eyes fly open wide. "I knocked him against the cage and when he rebounded back at me, I was waiting for him with a vicious hit. It pretty much separated his skull from his spine, internally, and he died right there."

Tears began to well up in his eyes and his voice trembled a bit. "So you see, son, while you are very very sad about the loss of your father, it was not your fault. He decided to drive fast. He decided. In my case, I killed my best friend because I decided. I decided that I didn't want to share my chance, my shot at glory, all the money and all the fame. I'd live homeless on the streets if I could take it all back and have my friend with me again. Through all your pain, all your feelings of loss, let go of your guilt. It will destroy you, as it has very nearly destroyed another relationship of mine." At that, he wept openly and hung his head. He became aware of them both clutching his hands while saying nothing. He wasn't sure how long it went on like that, but finally Bobby's mom spoke.

"Sounds like you two both need to forgive yourselves. I think you both need to make a promise, a vow. Both of you vow, to each other, let go of the guilt, let go of the unhappy thoughts of the dead. Let them go."

Bobby smiled awkwardly at Mel, "I vow."

"I vow too." Mel replied in kind.

There was a moment of silence as each absorbed the joy of releasing the burden they had carried.

"So," Bobby broke the silence, "think it's too late for me to qualify for State?" He was sincere, and Mel knew it.

"Kid, if you'll work hard and trust me, I guarantee you will make State. Whether you win the championship is up to you. That last bit of struggle and effort you'll need to be champion has to be inside you. I can't give you that. But I can get you to the dance, that's a promise."

"Deal. Whatever you say Coach Mel."

"OK. Show up tomorrow with purpose in your eyes. We will start molding mama's boy here in to a prospective state champion. Now, I have to go tell someone about my vow," he said with a big smile and wiped his eyes. He exchanged hugs with Bobby and his mom and headed for home.

When he pulled into the driveway and saw Terri's house lights were out, he was disappointed, but not dissuaded. He stopped right in front of the house, bounded up the front steps and began knocking on the door. He didn't stop knocking.

"What?! Dammit!! Stop knocking!" screamed Terri from inside. "Who's there?" she shouted as the porch light came on. "Oh, Mel," she said more softly, "hold on."

He turned the door knob and pushed the door open as soon as he heard the lock bolt slip open.

"Well, just come on in!" she seemed surprised. "What's going on?"

He stood there smiling and staring at her. "So I had a remarkable chat with Bobby and his mother."

"Ummm, OK, that's nice," she said in a sleepy voice. "I'm happy for you, and him. Yeah?"

"Yeah, but that's not why I woke you up."

"No?"

"No. Terri, did you ever forgive yourself for the porn movies you made?"

"I mostly did, but it wasn't complete really, until…. Until I knew you forgave me too."

"Did you forgive me for what I did in the cage? With…Phillip?"

"Of course, Mel. It was scary to see you like that, but I know that wasn't really you. Just like the girl on the screen wasn't really me. I lost myself. You lost yourself. I forgave you practically right away, but that doesn't matter, unless you can forgive yourself first."

"I have. Bobby and I sorta helped each other on that score. "

Suddenly her disposition changed to being more alert and curious. "What does that mean?"

"It means… it means I love you Terri. And if you'll give me a chance…"

She cut him off by throwing herself at him and silencing him with a kiss. A kiss that made their first one in the Tilt-O-Whirl look calm by comparison.

The next morning Lester rolled up to the house at his normal time and was surprised to see Mel's truck parked right outside. "Musta broke down," he muttered to himself. He went up the steps and knocked on the door but no one answered. He knocked again. Finally, Terri opened it and he walked in to the table at the front of the house where they always sat and planned their day. He was mildly surprised to see Mel already sitting there, but there were no cups of coffee on the table and he also noticed the coffee maker wasn't even doing its normal huffing and hissing. "What happened to your truck Mel? Did it stall?"

"Umm, no." he answered awkwardly.

Then Lester saw the two of them exchange a quick, furtive look at each other and then look away. And his gears began turning. First he grinned, then he smiled and then he started chuckling, "ooooohhhh you kids! You kids! Ha ha haaaaaaaaaaaaaaaaa…well, damn it's about time!"

Terri couldn't help herself and went over behind Mel, wrapped her arms around him and kissed him on the cheek, and he didn't resist in the least, only smiled.

Lester was still smiling. "Allright then, allright then! Ha haaaa!!! You guys just sit there and I'll make the coffee."

I Ran to Alva

Small Town Wildfire

Over the next three weeks, all was well. Mel and Terri were inseparable. Lester enjoyed watching their budding relationship because he'd known for at least 6 months they belonged together. And the wrestling team was plowing through their competition in ways that caught the town's attention for the first time ever. Of particular interest was Bobby Grayling's unbeaten streak and his march toward qualifying for the State Finals. It was the darkest part of the winter, but for many, the days were bright.

And then came the phone call.

"Mel, it's Doug. How are you today?"

"Doug! Never better sir! To what do I owe the pleasure of this call?" There was a prolonged silence that caught Mel's attention.

"I'd like you to come into the office, Doug. I need to talk with you about something in private."

"OK...when?"

"Well... the sooner the better, actually."

"Allright Doug. I'll be there in 15 minutes."

"What's that all about?" Lester asked when Mel shut the phone off.

"Not sure, but it didn't sound good. I gotta go. Tell Terri I went to the school, ok?"

"Sure."

When Mel arrived at the school, he went straight to Doug's office. The principal shook his hand but didn't have a smile for him. He closed the door behind Mel and then sat down with a somber expression on his face. "I'm obligated to inform you Mel that the sports boosters club has gathered enough signatures to force a hearing on whether you should be allowed to keep coaching the wrestling team."

"What?!?! Why?" He was bewildered.

"It seems that a student informed her guidance counselor that she had information about you that she believed the staff ought to know."

"Which was…?"

"Well, first of all, your overall background in cage fighting and most importantly, your behavior leading up to and during, the fight with Phillip Washington. I've seen several videos provided to me by members of the boosters club. I'm sure you know what I am talking about."

"I do."

"Mel, I do not support the booster club's action. I disapprove of cage fighting personally, but it is legal and growing in popularity. Furthermore what happened between you and Mr Washington was basically an accident, an unlucky strike. All your bluster may or may not have been real or may have been hyped up by the media, but it's irrelevant. You were never charged with a crime, or even arrested. Every now and then, a boxer dies in the ring, a football player dies on the field, and a race car driver dies on the track. It happens. If this issue were left to my sole authority, I would dismiss it, but the boosters gathered enough signatures to bring it before the school board and go over my head."

"What do I do now?"

"You can resign or you can appear before the school board and defend yourself, if you choose. You may also call up to 5 personal character witnesses to speak on your behalf. "

"Umm, OK, when is the meeting?"

"This Thursday."

"Three days??! Dammit Doug, the conference tournament is this weekend and Bobby Grayling begins the qualifier for the State Finals next weekend!"

"I know, Mel. I know. I cannot explain the rationale behind this. I think it's just blind fear and ignorance of that bourgeoning new sport and the fact that they don't know you. I will say this, if you decide to fight it, I'd be pleased if you asked me to be one of the five speakers. Ordinarily, I'd be voting on the issue, since I am a part of the board automatically, but in this case I am the one who hired you so I'm forbidden to vote on the decision."

This was the first good news Mel had heard on the issue. Having Doug in his corner would help tilt the scales, he was sure, but who else could he ask to speak for him? People who would really count? Terri? Lester? Maybe Coach Zack? Suddenly it occurred to him that he hadn't really made very many friends here. Always working or heading out for weekend jaunts with the ATV, or wrapped up in a wrestling activity of some sort. He had no idea if he could even find four more people that could speak for him in any meaningful way. That was troubling.

When he got back to the ranch, Terri came straight to him with obvious concern on her face. "Why did you have to go so suddenly?"

Mel told her the whole story and she seethed with anger. "They can't *do* that!" she said, practically spitting the words through her teeth. He was surprised at her intensity and had to smile in spite of himself. "What do you intend to do, Mel? Are you going to fight it? You have to fight it."

"Yeah of course, but honestly, except for Doug, who can I get to speak on my behalf that the board would know and take seriously? I'm still pretty new here; I don't know that many people."

"Well, I have made some community contacts; will you let me help you?"

"I'd be honored, Terri. Are you gonna stand by your man?" he quipped, making reference to the old Tammy Wynette song?

She unexpectedly kissed him and replied, "Stand by you, hell. I am going to plow the road. Just you watch. Just you watch."

Mel was not permitted to practice with the team until the hearing was done. This put the entire team, including Head

Coach Zack, in a state of mental disarray. Mel was hearing about all this through telephone updates and could barely work, so worried was he about the team. He needed to talk to them to calm them down, to remind them of the lessons on not getting rattled. Wednesday afternoon, several cars pulled into the driveway and stopped near the house. Mel was on the opposite side of the barn and came around when he heard the noise. All the members of the wrestling team were there, Coach Zack and a few parents.

"What's all this?" He asked.

"We're here to let you know that we will all be there tomorrow night for the hearing," Coach Zack said. "I heard you're allowed to have people speak on your behalf. I'd be honored if you'd let me."

Mel smiled and shook his hand. "Of course, thank you."

"And me," said Bobby, stepping forward. "Please let me speak for you Coach. You're about the only good thing that's happened to me since my dad died. Please let me speak for you," he concluded as his voice cracked and tears formed in his eyes.

Mel stepped forward and hugged Bobby. "Thank you son, I'd be honored. Now the rest of you... listen to me," he said with more authority in his voice. "Whatever happens tomorrow night is not as important as what you do this weekend. Keep your heads about you. Don't get rattled. Know your strategies, yes?"

"Yes..." they mumbled in reply.

"YES?" Mel shouted.

"YES!!!!" They screamed in unison.

"We all worked very hard this year and I am proud to be a part of this team. So proud. Now don't let that hard work go to waste. Keep practicing, keep your heads, make your season count and show the town something they can be proud of. Yes?"

"YES!!!" the ranch roared with the sound of their voices.

"Allright. I'll see you all tomorrow night then."

The driveway cleared out, except for Bobby. He stood silently, obviously needing to say something, but unsure how to start. Finally, "It was my little sister," he said.

"What do you mean, Bobby, what are you talking about?"

"My little sister, she is a freshman. She was down in her room the night you came out to the house. She only heard a small part of what we all talked about and she got the wrong idea. She was scared for me when she looked you up in the internet, so she told her guidance counselor. She told me all this yesterday. She's very sorry; she missed school today because she's so upset. She had no idea…"

Mel could only smile. What could he say? A little sister just trying to protect her brother from a "killer." Perfectly natural. "No worries, Bobby. In fact, do me a favor? Tell her you told me and tell her I said it's OK. It's OK."

Bobby could only nod his head, as he felt a bit ashamed to have to tell his coach that the entire impetus of this movement started with his own family. Bobby got in his old pickup and drove slowly out, but all Mel could think about was the boy's mindset and would he be focused enough for the conference tournament and the State Qualifier. It troubled him.

Mel walked with Terri into the high school gymnasium about 15 minutes before 7:00, the hearing's scheduled start time. He was stunned at the number of people in attendance and could only wonder how many were for or opposed to his firing. Terri patted his shoulder as she separated from him to go sit with her 4-H Troop and their parents. All of them had made signs, t-shirts, and painted their faces in support of Mel. He was deeply touched and gave them a grateful smile and a wave. He was also relieved to see Doug sitting with them. As he walked forward, he saw that Lester and Dylan Turner were already seated next to Coach Zack. Dylan's presence was a surprise to many and a source of much speculation. The first three rows of seats were all occupied by the wrestlers and their families. Then he caught a glimpse of Sheriff Peterson. Oh, yes, crowd control, Mel thought. This could get a bit heated, might be good to have the Sheriff in attendance. He quietly admonished the wrestlers to be orderly and be respectful, because if even one of them behaved poorly, it reflected on all of them as a team. They seemed to get the message, but he wasn't so sure.

Promptly at 7:00, the chairman banged the little gavel and brought the meeting to order. The crowd slowly quieted down and Mel thought the people around him could probably hear his heart pounding out of his chest. The chairman led the entire body of people through the pledge of allegiance and then sat down to business.

"Before us this evening is the matter of Assistant Wrestling Coach Dominic Melvin Hatcher and whether he has displayed moral turpitude to the point that he should be banned from participating in coaching our students. Per the board by-laws, the athletic boosters have presented the board with enough signatures to warrant this hearing. Boosters' President Merrillee Brown explained that they took this action instead of petitioning Principal Doug Sandoval on the matter, because it was in fact Principal Sandoval who hired Mr Hatcher, and thus they had concerns as to whether he would give the matter due consideration. This hearing shall proceed thus: Booster's President Brown shall present their case. They will be given as much as 15 minutes to do so. They may present information or evidence and they may call up to as many as 5 people who are not members of the boosters to buttress their case. Upon their conclusion, Mr Hatcher will be permitted 5 minutes to speak on his own behalf and to redress the complaints against him. At the end of 5 minutes, he may request additional time and the board must vote on whether or not to extend him another 5 minutes, but only one extension can be granted. Mr Hatcher will then be allowed to have up to 5 members of the community speak on his behalf. Upon the conclusion of those remarks, the board will be allowed up to 30 minutes to convene a recess, if necessary, to consider the matter before voting. Those who are familiar with these proceedings will note that Principal Sandoval is not seated here with the board tonight. That is in keeping with established precedent that the principal shall not be allowed to vote on any matter to which he was directly related. That leaves us with 6 voting members and runs the risk of a tie vote. In this case, the board members draw straws to see who will recuse themselves from the vote so that we have 5 voting members and thus have a majority decision, one way or the other. Board member Akins drew the short straw and may now step aside. Thank you Sherri. Do both parties understand the rules as I have explained them?"

Mel and Booster's President Brown both nodded.

"Good. Then let's proceed. During these proceedings, there will be no talking or making disruptions of any kind. As chairman, I have the authority to have any person removed from the room. I can in fact, declare a closed door session if it becomes necessary and throw everyone out. And, interestingly enough, we have Sheriff Peterson here tonight in case that becomes necessary. Good to see you Sheriff, thank you for coming by."

The Sheriff merely nodded. Mel was puzzled. It was obvious that the Chairman had not expected him to be there. Why not?

"Ms Brown, you may begin."

Over the course of the next 15 minutes, Mel sat and squirmed in his chair while the pious and pompous woman he'd never met impugned him personally and all cage fighters universally. She even had a couple YouTube videos spooled up on her computer which she'd already connected to the large wheeled television monitor. During the playback of the videos, there were audible gasps and shrieks from the audience and even a couple of the board members. This was not going well. He felt sweat forming on his forehead and had to remind himself not to get rattled. He knew his boys would be watching. OK, he told himself, prepare for your counter attack, and fight for what you want. He was so zoned into his own world that he was not even aware she had finished until he heard a few people in the audience applauding.

"Mr Hatcher, you may proceed."

Mel presented cogent and accurate data on injuries and deaths from all manner of sports since such statistics had begun to be collected. He was able to show, factually, that deaths in cage fighting were no greater than boxing and were 15 times less common than, of all things, horseback riding. That drew a few chuckles from the crowd because they all knew Merrillee Brown was a renowned horse trainer. On the personal side, Mel laid bare his feelings. He gave a history of his relationship with Phillip, had a couple pictures of them together in happier days. The timer chimed the end of his 5 minutes and he asked for an extension. Much to his surprise and to the surprise of everyone in the hearing, he was denied. This gave Mel a sinking feeling, as if the whole thing was already a fait accompli, a done deal, and it was all a charade to make it look legal.

"But you may ask your 5 representatives to speak for you now," the board chairman allowed.

Coach Zack spoke first and he talked of a transformation in the wrestling team in every way a team can be transformed. He attributed it all to Mel instructing the boys on how to make good decisions and how to be responsible for their bad ones. Much of what he said talked up Mel's personal character, but Mel saw it had no effect. The board members' eyes were collectively glazed over, they were not listening.

Ditto when Bobby Grayling presented. His story was a bit more touching and had some members of the audience wiping their eyes as he recounted his father's untimely death. He recounted for them how Mel took the time to come see him, to encourage him and he gave all credit to Mel for his unbeaten streak since that time, but Mel saw it in their faces.. not listening.

Doug stood, with all the authority and gravitas as principal, and made personal observations about Mel from the perspective of a clinically trained psychologist. That was a great big surprise to Mel, but it was comforting to know that a board certified shrink did not consider him to be a violent, homicidal maniac. Still, the board members' apathy was plain as their collective noses. They could probably count the seconds until it was time to "vote."

Then came Dylan's turn. The big man, who was so imposing and arrogant to so many in attendance, was noticeably awkward and nervous. Mel saw that the board members' curiosity was piqued as each of them leaned a bit forward in their chairs and stopped scribbling or doodling on the papers in front of them.

"M-many of you know me," he started with a trembling voice, "and most of you have a low opinion of me." The gymnasium hummed quietly with the hushed comments of people muttering agreement. "I earned that low opinion, I know. I made some bad choices when I was a kid, flunked out of college and wasted an opportunity to make a better life for myself. Since then, I've practically made an art form of being an ass and a bully." Some muted laughter followed that remark. "What you don't know is that recently I've begun to see myself through your eyes. And that started because of something that happened between Mel and me. I attempted to bully him like I have done to some of you in this gym and it didn't work out so well," he concluded with a quick laugh. "He put me on the ground three times and barely broke a sweat doing it. He could have hurt me, could have injured me out of spite and there was nothing I could do to stop it." The entire gym was now buzzing and Lester caught Mel's eye. The two men exchanged a glance confirming Lester's suspicions, but Mel just shrugged at him. "None of you ever heard about that event until now, because Mel is not a braggart, never breathed a word of it, and I sure as hell wasn't going to say anything." The gym resonated with laughter. "But his sense of fairness, or mercy, is greater even than his fighting ability, as I learned firsthand. Some of you just now watched an edited video of Mel in a situation you know nothing about and drew certain conclusions as to his fighting skills and his savagery. I'm here to tell you first hand that he has more control over his temper than any man I've ever met. His ability to put me down, his decision to not hurt me in a situation I created, and willingness to protect my dignity by not talking about it, caused me to wonder about him. I had to wonder about a guy with that much fighting ability and yet that much self-control, and it actually caused me to admire him a little and wonder if maybe one day we might become friends. Yet I realized for that to happen, I'd have to be a different guy. I'd have to change. No way would a guy like Mel ever be friends with a guy like me, so I am not that guy anymore. Actually, I haven't been for a while now. You people on this board have known me all my life and know what an ass I can be. I'm here to tell you that I am not that man anymore and the reason for it is because of the man you're presently considering firing. I think that would be a huge mistake on your part. Thank you." The gym was slowly but steadily filled with applause as Dylan turned to take his seat. He smacked Mel hard on the shoulder and the two men exchanged a smile for all to see. The chairman banged the gavel repeatedly and reminded everyone to remain quiet.

Last it was time for Terri. She described how she might not have hired Mel if she had gleaned everything about his background right from the get go. On paper, she conceded, he might look like trouble, but he had proven to be a patient, hard worker and honest to a fault as she briefly told the story about the money from the scrap metal. She asked that the board extend forgiveness of the same magnitude that Mel had given to her. The board members seemed confused at her statement and Mel saw where this was going.

"Terri, no, you don't have to say anything! They'll cut you down too!" Mel pleaded with her as he looked back at the now-confused 4-H troop. She ignored him.

"Mel loves me and is in love with me and I pray he will love me the rest of my life. Before he could love me, he had to forgive me of something in my past, too. Something worse than anyone in this room is guilty of, I am sure. Several years ago, I performed in six pornographic films over a span of 18 months."

The entire gym erupted in gasps and "what's?". Even Lester sat up in surprise.

She continued, unfazed. "That period of my life wrecked me. I fled that life and for a couple years, had no roots, nowhere to go. Always running from my past until, by chance or by God's grace, I ran here, to Alva. The quiet decency and the hard

221

working mindset of this community is truly a spectacle to behold when you've seen the underbelly of Los Angeles and New York, as I have. This community helped me to slowly find myself again, to stop running, to find a place I could call home, but this man before you did more than all of you could do together. He forgave me my past and let me heal. If this board cannot extend the same courtesy to him, then I question whether you have the human capacity necessary for educating and nurturing children."

She turned defiantly from the podium and the entire room erupted in wild, supportive applause. She took a chair next to Mel and sat with her shoulders squared and her chin high. Even though Mel suspected she'd lose half her contracts and her role with the 4-H troop, she had never looked so beautiful. She turned to look at him and he stared again into those eyes. He felt down deep that this hearing and his effort to keep his coaching job was a lost cause, but he knew he'd be alright now, looking into her eyes. It would be Ok. "The rest of your life, huh?" he yelled so she could hear.

"All or nothing cowboy! You need to man up for the long haul or leave now," She replied, but with a twinkle in those beautiful eyes.

"I ain't going anywhere!"

The board chairman ceaselessly pounded the gavel in an effort to quiet the crowd, to no avail. Chants of "Hat-chet!... Hat-chet!... Hat-chet! " broke out spontaneously and of all things, the 4-H girls and their moms were on their feet screaming "Terrrreeeeeee!!!! We love yoooooooooouuuuuuu!!!!!" Much to the chairman's relief, Sheriff Peterson stood up, walked toward the podium and then faced the crowd with his hands up.

Mel spoke into Terri's ear. "Sorry, sweety, but this doesn't look like it's gonna go our way. Thank you, though," he concluded as he kissed the side of her face.

"Don't be so sure," she replied as she turned to look at him. "Remember what I said about plowing the road?"

Mel nodded.

"The plow is about to roll," she said, nodding toward the standing sheriff.

The crowd settled down and Sheriff Peterson turned to face the board.

"Thank you Sheriff Peterson," the chairman acknowledged. "Now since we have heard from all five…"

"I'd like to say something with the board's permission," the Sheriff cut him off.

The chairman was surprised, but receptive. "Of course."

"I graduated from the Maryland State Police Academy 32 years ago. The City of Baltimore hired me onto their police force and one year later, I was involved in my first shooting. My partner and I pulled over a car with two young black men in it. I had been trained, officially, to be more wary and suspicious of black people than whites. My own father's prejudicial attitude about blacks had also rubbed off on me all the years I was growing up. Suffice to say, I was not a proponent of diversity in my youth, or as a young cop. Anyway, my partner instructed the two men to get out of the car and they complied. We had our revolvers trained on them the entire time and they knew it. I was covering the passenger and was asking him questions from a few feet away. His answers to my questions seemed incoherent and he tried to tell me that he had been sick. Given my attitude toward black men at the time, I figured he was just hyped up on some dope or other and was making up the story to explain his behavior. He reached toward his jacket pocket, claiming that he could show me his prescription. The second his hand went inside the pocket, I pulled the trigger and killed him."

He paused momentarily to compose himself and the room was so quiet that each person could hear their own breathing.

"Sure enough, the only thing in his pocket was a bottle of prescription antibiotics. I was cleared of any wrong doing because we had warned him to keep his hands in plain sight at all times. Being sick as he was, maybe he was just a little fuzzy in the head, but he died... because... of me... and my prejudices." He paused and the board members could see the tears beginning to roll down his cheeks. The audience could see from behind that his breathing was a little convulsive as he tried to keep himself composed. "If he'd been a white kid, I'd have given him... the benefit of the doubt. I'd have given him... half a second to reach into that pocket and present the bottle, but because he was black, I shot first." He sobbed, "I shot first... and took his life. I could only stand another couple months in that environment before I had to get away. I know this will come as a surprise to many of you, but the previous Sheriff, Mason Torrrance, was my uncle." That revelation did set many tongues wagging in the room. "He told me to come out here and he'd bring me on his deputy staff. Back in those days, there was no internet, no way for the common citizen to look up someone and dig into their background. So the only background check done on me was done by my uncle, the sitting Sheriff. Ten years later, he died while still in office and the County appointed me acting Sheriff until the next election. You fine people in this county have had the decency to re-elect me ever since, but there was a time that I also had something to hide, and something to run from. So, like the lovely Terri Green and the upstanding Dominic Melvin Hatcher, I too ran here, to Alva. You people have trusted me to serve as your sheriff for more than 20 years now. I've never been indicted, subpoenaed or even failed an audit, because I run a squeaky clean ship. That's just how I believe a police outfit ought to be run; from my heart I believe that. My heart used to be a dark place. Over time, it was healed, I was healed and many of you people were instrumental in that. In return, I believe I have earned your trust and served you well. I am asking that the community at large do the same for Mel and Terri, and this board should specifically extend that trust to Mr Dominic Melvin Hatcher. Thank you." He quietly stepped away from the podium and toward the exit door. Applause started politely, then grew louder and louder and louder until there was a tsunami of sound. Hands clapped, feet stomped, those who could whistle, did so, and loudly.

The chairman pounded and pounded and pounded the gavel, to no avail and the Sheriff had left the gym. Finally, in frustration, the chairman turned and drew all the board members close enough so he could shout at them. Yet the crowd did not relent. The wrestlers were on their feet, led by Head Coach Zack, chanting "Hat-chet! Hat-chet! Hat-chet!" and pumping their fists in the air. The rest of the crowd simply continued creating as many decibels as humanly possible. For a moment, Mel began to wonder if he shouldn't have just resigned. These people all knew each other and would have to live together. He was a relative stranger who had come in and caused all this chaos. Terri bumped his shoulder to get his attention. She pointed to the board members arguing and had a small, tight smile on her lips. While Mel had been looking around at all the chaos, her eyes never left the proceedings and on several occasions, she made eye contact with them. Now he was also observing a very tense argument among the board members, but not a word of which could be heard over the cacophony.

Suddenly the chairman angrily dismissed the group. He leaned into the microphone and screamed, "By a vote of three to two, the motion to dismiss Coach Hatcher is denied!" and then walked away in a huff. Just when Mel thought the place could not get any louder, it did. Terri prompted him to stand and wave to everyone, so he did, and then he looked at her a good long while before he kissed her. He muttered thank you to her but he knew she couldn't hear. Still, he was certain she got the message. The crowd remained in the gym, celebrating their win and lauding their new hero. Finally, Doug came over and asked Mel if he would start walking toward the door, because the crowd was going to stay as long as he did. Mel laughed about it and hugged the Principal in gratitude, then took Terri's hand toward the exit.

Outside, Molly, Sarah and the rest of the 4-H troop and parents were waiting. Terri saw them, smiled at first but then froze. The fear set in, what would they say? Did they feel betrayed by the adult film whore who had chaperoned their daughters? The weight of it was coming down on her now and she started to tear up. She looked at Molly and could barely get the words out. "I'm sorry Molly….. I'm sorry Sarah…….. I never meant……. to lie to you. I'm sorry…..to all of you. I'm so sorry."

"Oh honeyyyyyyyy," Molly crooned. "Do you know how Doug and I met?"

"Ugh!" Sarah protested, "Are you gonna tell this story again??!"

"I'll keep it brief. Terri, I met Doug when he was doing his grad work at UNLV. I was also working in Vegas and I met him where I worked – at a strip club. We all can change honey. I think I speak for all the moms and the girls when I tell you we think you are a wonderful woman and a terrific 4-H leader and we don't want you to go anywhere."

Terri was so overjoyed that she was unable to speak. Tears flowed down her face as the girls all moved in to hug her. She looked at Mel and gave him a trembling smile. He wondered if he could make her that happy the rest of her life.

I Ran to Alva

More Pictures for Ruby

The locals in Ruby's diner still like to talk about all that
unfolded during that winter and spring. The raucous hearing
when the school board almost removed The Hatchet (as they
affectionately called him) from the wrestling coach position,
and then how the wrestling team went to the conference
tournament and began their dynasty. Ruby had their team pic
on the wall with each of their signatures. She could recite all
their names and tell stories about their parents. She could point
to Bobby Grayling's individual picture on the wall next to them
and recite perfectly how he became conference champ, which
qualified him for the state tournament that he also went on to
win.

But one of her very favorite pictures in the whole place was
from Mel and Terri's wedding day. The two of them seated
backwards on the little Ford tractor, smiling bright and pointing
at the little sign fastened to the seat "No more running."

THE END

About the Author:

Jack Randy Martin's life experiences allow him to bring a wide variety of personalities, places, occupations, relationships and hobbies into his stories and characters. He was born in Texas, raised in the wilds of Upper Michigan, schooled in Ohio and has lived his adult life in California. In this journey, he has worked as paperboy, ice cream server, tour guide, truck stop attendant, pipeline worker, radar/avionics engineer, limousine chauffeur, computer software engineer and author. He is an adoptee and a cancer survivor, married 25 years with 5 children, 5 cats, 4 dogs, 3 sheep, 2 goats and a dove. Somewhere between career and family, he has managed to be a motorcycle racer, marathoner and triathlete. His love for motorcycles led him to become a columnist for Examiner.com where he has published more than 200 articles. His first novel, I Ran to Alva, is the culmination of an idea that took 15 years to transpire, though it was actually written in one month. Each of his stories covers a diverse range of places, people and events, but with one underlying theme. For one story that theme will be guilt, for another forgiveness and another perseverance. These and other core sentiments live in the heart of every human being, rich or poor, young or old, male or female, atheist or believer, and it is the exploration of these core sentiments that comprises the foundations of Jack Randy Martin's stories.

Made in the USA
San Bernardino, CA
23 November 2013